Measuring Institutional
Performance
in
Higher Education

Measuring Institutional Performance in Higher Education

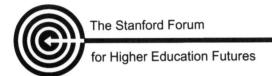

The Stanford Forum
for Higher Education Futures

Joel W. Meyerson and William F. Massy
Editors

Peterson's

Princeton, New Jersey

Library of Congress Cataloging-in-Publication Data

Measuring institutional performance in higher education / Joel W. Meyerson and
   William F. Massy, editors.
       p.   cm.
     "The theme of this year's Stanford Forum for financing higher education
  futures was 'Measuring institutional performance'"—Introd.
   Includes bibliographical references.
   ISBN 1-56079-331-7
   1. Education, Higher—United States—Administration—Evaluation—
Congresses. 2. Universities and colleges—United States—Finance—
Evaluation—Congresses. 3. Educational accountability—United States—
Congresses. 4. Educational indicators—United States—Congresses.
I. Meyerson, Joel W., 1951–   . II. Massy, William F.
LB2341.M367   1993
378'.1'00973—dc20   93-6403
                                                CIP

Composition and design by Peterson's

Printed in the United States of America

10 9 8 7 6 5 4 3 2 1

Contents ———————————————

Preface

The Stanford Forum for Higher Education Futures is a national research center resident at Stanford University. Its mission is to improve the strategy, finance, and management of American colleges and universities. The Stanford Forum helps college and university officers and governing boards respond to new imperatives, develop viable institutional strategies, and implement them through effective finance and management. It conducts and sponsors research and disseminates knowledge through symposia, retreats, books, and monographs. Forum fellows include leaders and innovators in higher education and industry. The Stanford Forum is the successor to the Forum for College Financing, which was resident at Columbia University.

Introduction

Change in Higher Education: Its Effect on Institutional Performance

Joel W. Meyerson and Sandra L. Johnson

"Measuring Institutional Performance" immediately calls to mind ratios, models, and other mathematical analyses—and such quantitative measurements are key. But at this point in higher education's evolution, the underlying theme of change is pervasive. Although each of the papers in this book incorporates measurement tools, the notion of the radical change that is transforming the higher education environment today is equally evident.

The list of changes is extensive: increasing operating costs, decreasing and more volatile revenue sources, increasing calls for accountability from government and others, and public disillusionment with higher education are a sample. Clearly, change is happening to colleges and universities just as it sweeps through the external economic, social, and political environment. The question remains: Is higher education responding sufficiently to change? The answer may be, as this introduction suggests, that the internal management and organizational changes that are needed are substantial, while the changes that are occurring at many institutions are tentative.

In either case, measuring performance is a key component of change; it is a way to compare where an institution is with where it strives to be in reaction to or anticipation of change.

Colleges and universities are certainly not the only institutions in our society affected by change. Management visionary Peter Drucker commented on the pace of change in our society in *Managing for the Future: The 1990s and Beyond*: "In a crafts society, which ours essentially was until late in the nineteenth century, major changes occurred perhaps every 80 years. . . . Today . . . it is probably every 60 days. The acceleration of change in our society is something we all must find ways to deal with, in our personal and professional lives, as well as in the organizations we manage."[1]

DEFINING INSTITUTIONAL PERFORMANCE

Changing an organization involves developing new ways to assess and measure its performance. Measuring performance is not a one-time-only activity but rather should be continuous. It is a way to continually assess where an organization wants to be—which often changes as new goals are reached—and where it is. It follows that if an institution is undergoing significant change, then the way it measures its financial performance should also change, perhaps to capture the progress of new initiatives or to present its current financial resources for change more completely.

Ideally, a measurement system should be simple and easy to understand, involve in its development many constituencies in the institution, measure what is most important, and be continually improved.

Setting important goals—those that are the prerequisites for future success—and appropriately measuring performance toward their achievement—by obtaining the right information and setting good benchmarks—are key, according to Robert Scott, Vice President for Finance at Harvard University, in "Measuring Performance in Higher Education." He uses two examples from Harvard to illustrate these points.

One of the university's goals has been to develop financial reports that were more useful to readers, measured the true cost of facilities, and addressed more completely significant financial liabilities. Harvard wanted to be able to answer in its financial statements the question "Did we have a good year?" After much analysis the university determined that if, after all expenses were accrued—including those related to plant renewal—and after adjusting for inflation, net assets had grown sufficiently to support current program operations and future plans, it had been a good year. In 1991 the university's financial reports were changed to reflect its needs, generating much discussion in the higher education community. Harvard's future goals include continuing to refine its budgeting process so that the full cost of plant maintenance is reflected.

Second, the university wanted to determine if its financial aid strategy was working. Harvard considered four interrelated factors: the cost of a degree, the net cost to a student after scholarship aid, the student's starting salary at graduation, and the student's debt level at graduation. The university developed a computer model to consider various alternatives and concluded that a rational student aid policy would include, among other components, more scholarship aid for students who received lower starting salaries and, conversely, less scholarship aid for students who received higher starting salaries.

MEASURING EDUCATIONAL PERFORMANCE

William Massy of Stanford University discusses accountability and educational performance measurement from the perspective of the research institution in "Measuring Performance: How Colleges and Universities Can Set Meaningful Goals and Be Accountable." He asserts that institutional prestige has come from research rather than teaching, but that the process has gone too far. When graphed, research improves educational quality at first, but later, educational quality and research become substitutes. The result of overemphasizing research is an increase in the cost per student, the proliferation of support services, and less quality time for undergraduates from faculty. Massy's thesis is that institutions must develop a better balance between the resources they allocate to research and those they allocate to teaching.

Massy then discusses measuring teaching quality. In effect, teaching is the delivery of a service. Three conditions help ensure excellence in service delivery:

- The service provider must care about the client—who is in this case the student—engage fully in the task of teaching and do his or her best to adapt to the student's needs.

- The service provider must request feedback and use it to improve his or her performance.

- A coherent curriculum is also necessary.

Massy's chapter includes a table depicting actions that faculty work groups and institutions could take to promote good undergraduate teaching. For example, faculty work groups could establish goals and incentives for continuing professional education of faculty in teaching skills, and they could regularly assess teaching programs through feedback from students and peers. Institutions could reward exemplary teaching and include teaching skills as one of the criteria for promotion and tenure. Massy adds that "colleges and universities do not lack ways to assess progress toward educational quality—in fact, there may be an embarrassment of riches."

COMPARING CORPORATE AMERICA AND HIGHER EDUCATION

Colleges and universities are distinctly singular institutions. However, some of the changes occurring in American business today may be relevant to higher education. Prescriptions for restructuring corporate America bear remarkable similarity to those for higher education. In many respects the challenges higher education faces and the challenges corporate America faces are more alike than different.

For example, Rosabeth Moss Kanter, an authority on change in corporate America, cites the phrase "do more with less" as a prescription for corporate America in the 1990s.[2] How many times have we heard "do more with less" in higher education? Although it rings true, it has become one of the most overused phrases in higher education. And it appears to apply as much to corporate America as it does to higher education.

Tom Peters, another noted authority on corporate American management, provides several other similarities. Peters's description of the successful firm of the 1990s and beyond could very well be a description of the successful college or university in the 1990s and beyond. According to Peters,[3] the successful firm will need to:

- Differentiate and become a niche player
- Be recognized as a provider of quality service
- Be responsive to the customer
- Be innovative in functional areas (i.e., accounting, personnel, etc.), develop new ways of doing things, and eliminate bureaucratic rules that impede action-taking
- Empower employees and listen to them
- Simplify and reduce the organizational structure and rely more on a team approach to management
- Lead with an inspiring vision

Regarding this last point, Peters quotes a former president of Notre Dame University, Father Theodore Hesburgh, who said: "The very essence of leadership is that you have to have a vision. It's got to be a vision you articulate clearly and forcefully on every occasion. You can't blow an uncertain trumpet."[4]

The notion of visionary leadership is echoed by Francis Gouillart, a senior international consultant with Gemini Consulting, who describes his experience working with industry in "The Self-Transformation of Corporations: A Lesson from Industry." Recalling many of the themes found in a review of corporate management literature—including those of Peter Drucker and Rosabeth Moss Kanter discussed above—Gouillart describes three dimensions of business transformation: (1) the reframing of corporate issues, (2) the restructuring of the company and the accompanying redesign of the work processes, and (3) the revitalization of the organization.

Gouillart suggests that one of the toughest challenges in business transformation is convincing people that change is necessary. Each successful corporate transformation carries the signature of a leader who informs the change with purpose as well as provides a process for its accomplishment. Reframing corporate issues requires the leadership of someone who can articulate for the company far-reaching goals and a winning strategy.

In Gouillart's prescription for restructuring the company he echoes the words of many modern theorists who contend that change is the one constant of our modern economic world. Restructuring proceeds continuously along two dimensions: (1) adjusting the asset base of the corporation, and (2) process reengineering. Process reengineering is a concept heard frequently in higher education today. It involves examining the way processes unfold in an organization and rethinking how they lead to the accomplishment of an organization's functions and activities.

Gouillart also discusses revitalizing the organization. This involves making operational improvements that affect revenue. Because of the early and cautious efforts by Japanese managers to improve quality and service, they can now focus on enhancing revenues, while American and European CEOs stress quality and service as their first priorities. Although Gouillart questions what the different priorities of American, European, and Japanese managers might mean to American business, the relative ordering of these priorities in American higher education remains to be seen.

Like American business, higher education is becoming increasingly concerned with quality and service, although most institutions have only begun to discuss these concepts and have yet to implement broad-based quality and service initiatives. Like industry, some institutions have established "business" process reengineering programs, and many more recognize the need to do so. Most American colleges and universities are focusing on improving their financial performance, typically by reducing costs. This contrasts considerably with the ways that American industry is trying to improve its financial performance, according to Gouillart. He notes industry's focus on enhancing revenue by creating new businesses and by buying and selling pieces of the corporate entity—options that are largely unavailable to colleges and universities.

MEASURING FINANCIAL PERFORMANCE

Financial performance measures for colleges and universities and the changes that are occurring with financial statement presentation in higher education are the focus of Williams College's Gordon Winston. He discusses the concept of "global accounts," which he defines as a simple and "idealized aggregate (financial) account," in "New Dangers in Old Traditions: The Reporting of Economic Performance in Colleges and Universities." While traditional college and university fund accounting focuses only on financial wealth, global accounting incorporates an additional element—an institution's physical wealth. For example, Williams College had approximately $309 million in financial wealth (e.g., endowment, cash, investments, and other traditional fund accounting measures) in 1991, but approximately $644 million when the replacement value of plant, equipment, and land was included.

Global accounts are particularly useful as the basis for developing an economic plan for an institution. Global accounting answers such questions as:

- How much money did the institution take in during the year?
- How was the money spent?
- What effect did its spending and saving have on the institution's real wealth?

Knowing the financial status of an institution in these basic terms facilitates planning. For example, if an institution's plant is not maintained, its market value—and hence the economic value of the entire institution—falls. Global accounting focuses attention squarely on yearly saving and spending. At its most basic level, saving increases wealth (for future generations), while spending reduces wealth (using it on the present generation).

A NEW VISION FOR HIGHER EDUCATION

Change, especially radical change, is sometimes difficult to think about and can be even more difficult to experience. You get used to operating in a certain way, having the people around you respond in expected ways, and feeling the institution you work for represents stability. You may take comfort in the fact that your college or university has been there for many years and will be there for many more to come. For most institutions that is probably true.

The question is: What will colleges and universities look like in five years? In ten years? As this introduction suggests, today's corporate—and higher education—world is all about change, and the organizations we work for today are likely to be very different by the year 2000.

In his *Harvard Business Review* article "The New Society of Organizations," Peter Drucker commented: "Similarly, it is a safe prediction that in the next 50 years, schools and universities will change more and more drastically than they have since they assumed their present form more than 300 years ago when they reorganized themselves around the printed book. What will force these changes is, in part, new technology, such as computers, videos, and telecasts via satellite; in part the demands of a knowledge-based society in which organized learning must become a lifelong process for knowledge workers; and in part new theory about how human beings learn."[5]

If such radical change is to occur, colleges and universities will have to restructure administratively as well as academically. Benchmarking, Total Quality Management (TQM), and Business Process Reengineering (BPR) are vehicles for accomplishing change, sometimes radical change, particularly in the administrative functions of an organization. Increasingly, however, academic activities are candidates for benchmarking, TQM, and BPR.

TQM and BPR are methods that focus not only on meeting customer needs and expectations but also on the process by which goods and services are provided to customers. They also stress objectively measuring such variables as customer satisfaction, timeliness of delivery, and service. Benchmarking involves identifying competitors that exemplify "best practices" in some function or process and then comparing one's own performance to this standard. The process can be eye-opening, making boards and management aware of ways of doing things they had not thought possible. Benchmarking, TQM, and BPR have been used by industry and are now making their way into higher education.

Sean Rush, a higher education partner at Coopers & Lybrand, discusses benchmarking in "Benchmarking—How Good is Good?" He describes benchmarking as a way to provide an institution with a yardstick for measuring its cost or quality advantage over its competitors. Benchmarking is used—often in conjunction with BPR and TQM—to dramatically change how institutions view themselves and how they conduct their activities.

Traditionally, colleges and universities have focused on cost inputs, equating greater dollars spent with higher quality. Departments compete for more of the budgetary pie each year, arguing that they can achieve more. Benchmarking focuses instead on output. It measures how well a department produces its service and for what cost. Reframing department expenditures to focus on outputs rather than inputs is increasingly critical as institutional budgets are reduced. The primary objective for the vast majority of institutions today is to reduce costs as revenue sources become increasingly constrained and less predictable.

Let's consider a hypothetical example. If a university spends $37 to process an admission application, and it typically processes 13,000 applications, its average annual cost for that activity is $481,000. If the university processes 57,000 purchase orders at a cost of $26 per transaction, it spends almost $1.5 million annually to accomplish this task. If the university could reduce its transaction costs for just these two activities by 30 percent, it would save approximately $590,000 per year.

Benchmarking is one method for accomplishing this objective. It allows our hypothetical university to discover: (1) whether its transaction cost of $26 per purchase order is, in fact, good, and (2), if others are performing the same activity for less, how their processes can be adopted or adapted at the university. In addition, the university may learn that not only are its peers spending less to process a purchase order, they also are accomplishing this task in 10 days instead of 20. If the university can improve the way it processes purchase orders, it will save money *and* enhance the quality of its service.

MANAGING CHANGE AND MEASURING SHORT-TERM PERFORMANCE

Many presidents and CFOs today are attempting to work with change and build into their institutions the capacity for quickly adapting to it. This is becoming increasingly important as the tenure of senior executives at colleges and universities shortens. Just a few years ago, the president of a university, for example, typically served for about ten years; today that tenure is approximately seven years. This trend toward shorter terms—and the enormity of the challenge facing some institutions—compels presidents to quickly assess the situation and start making needed changes. Many new presidents find they must take early, decisive action—often without the benefit of extensive analysis—to establish new leadership and to show that change will occur.

Such was the challenge faced by Linda Wilson, the new president of Radcliffe College, and Nancy Dunn, the college's new chief financial officer. Like most new senior executives today, they arrived at a critical juncture in their institution's history; resources were scarce, and the role of Radcliffe within the Harvard community was under debate. Although the relationship of Radcliffe College and Harvard University is unique, many of the challenges the college's new president and CFO faced are typical to many new administrations. Therefore, the questions President Wilson and now Vice President Dunn address in their joint chapter "Strategic Shortcuts for Short-Term Success" are widely relevant to higher education senior executives.

At Radcliffe the board expected the new president to serve the college well (e.g., affecting constituents in positive ways and increasing the value ascribed to the college) and to manage well (e.g., developing and managing resources effectively). With these broad expectations before them and little time to analyze the situation in depth, Linda Wilson and Nancy Dunn used three strategic shortcuts.

The first was the "Rainbow," a technique to organize and prioritize goals, objectives, and responsibilities. To get an idea of the power of this relatively simple model, visualize the bands of a rainbow. The top band represents the institutional mission, while succeeding bands represent key goals, objectives, tasks, and subtasks that help support the mission and achieve the goals at hand. The president's role is to manage the authorizing environment, the top two bands of the rainbow, while the vice president's role, with the help of her staff, is to accomplish the supportive tasks of the other bands in the rainbow. Keeping this model in mind helps keep senior management on track, reducing the chances of micromanaging every task.

The second tool was the "Triangle," which helps identify conflicts between expectations and circumstances and helps adjust the pace of change. The triangle gathers in one place the mission statement, external forces, and internal resources available to accomplish an objective. More importantly, it helps to visualize the sometimes contradictory forces affecting an objective and to determine how to offset opposition by deploying resources strategically.

The third tool was "multiple, partial converging indicators," a measurement device borrowed from science. Indicators of success in science—and in management—are often difficult to isolate; but when several variables, or partial converging indicators, point in the same direction, the possibility of success becomes greater. Given limited time for analysis, partial converging indicators suggest either that the chosen course of action is working or that revisions are necessary.

President Wilson and Vice President Dunn have found that these three techniques, or "strategic shortcuts," have helped them manage their transition to Radcliffe College and measure short-term performance.

PERFORMANCE MEASUREMENT FOR TRUSTEES

In addition to the chapters that appear in this book, the Stanford Forum for Higher Education Futures explored the relationship between trustees and senior financial officers in measuring performance from several different perspectives—that of the public university, the large private institution (often a research institution), and the smaller private institution. The overall objective was to suggest performance measures that would enable boards to be more effective.

Public Universities

The role of boards within public institutions differs dramatically from private institution boards. For example, certain public boards are appointed by the governor; others are elected, often representing a political party or geographic area of the state. Advisory boards have limited authority, while boards with state constitutional authority have far greater powers. Board size may vary greatly as well, creating different information as well as structural needs. For example, the University of New Hampshire board has over thirty members, while the University of Michigan board has only eight members. Multicampus boards, such as that of SUNY, function very differently from single-campus boards of trustees. Perhaps the most far-reaching difference is that public university boards face greater public scrutiny than do the boards of private institutions.

Given this diversity in boards and their public nature, it is difficult to design generic approaches to effective board discussions of performance measurements, restructuring initiatives, and change. However, several general statements can be made. First, trustees should focus on mission, as defined by three questions:

- Where do we want to go?
- Where are we?
- Who are we?

The public institution's mission and how these three questions are answered will vary significantly depending on the nature of the board. Again, board diversity (political, geographical, appointed, elected, multicampus, single-campus, etc.) plays a very critical role in public university governance.

Second, public trustees need to develop an internal process to enable them to make necessary but difficult decisions. This process may need to be more well-defined than that of private boards. The tenure of the chairman on a public university board—who often sets the tone of the group, elicits discussion, and personally influences the decision-making process—may be quite short; many public institutions represented at the Stanford Forum had boards whose chairs change annually. This means that the board must develop a decision-making process that is not dependent on the chairman.

Third, public boards often have many legally or statutorily required items on their agendas, creating another impediment to tackling restructuring, performance measurement, mission, or change. Public boards may need to conduct planning sessions separate from business meetings or establish subcommittees to discuss strategic issues.

Fourth, public universities are often driven by their annual budgets, making it difficult to address issues of long-term financial health. In addition, the budget process usually is driven by the academic side of the university. For these reasons, it is critical for the CEO to bring academic and financial officers together to discuss performance criteria jointly.

Large Private Institutions

The involvement of board members in large private institutions also varies considerably. Some boards are very involved in the direction of the institution; others grant more of that responsibility to the president. Boards that take a hands-on approach may request in-depth data on the institution's strengths and weaknesses, and on occasion may challenge institutional policies. An active board is preferred by many higher education senior executives; many view an active board as an ally that understands "business" realities. However, the full knowledge and consent of the president is a necessary ingredient in any alliance between senior institutional administration and the board.

The role of the CFO, especially with an active board, is to educate the board. He or she should provide regular, consistent reports that "demystify" data. Active, informed board members can be valuable in evaluating schools or departments, and constructive criticism is often welcomed by senior executives in higher education.

Small Private Institutions

In addition to its financial and fund-raising role, the board of a small private institution is entrusted with two key roles. The first is its fiduciary role, and the second is its role in critiquing constructively the strategic direction and operations of the institution. Inherent in these roles is the board's charge to work toward the institution's financial equilibrium.

What should be the role of the CFO in providing guidance and information to the board? Here are some suggestions:

- Don't overload the board with detail
- Use expenditures as the key control mechanism (revenues, on the other hand, are fairly straightforward, and budgets are subject to management discretion)
- Tie information to the institution's strategic goals and objectives

In terms of the type of information to present to the board, the CFO should focus on key areas, presenting data on the change in revenues and expenditures, the endowment spending rate, and the physical plant. In terms of what type of analysis to present to the board, key ratios measuring liquidity, performance, and wealth are generally considered to be the most important, along with "economic" data on enrollment and market share.

CONCLUSION

The chapters in this book stress that *measuring institutional performance* in the 1990s includes assessing financial, educational, and overall institutional performance in new ways; being accountable for institutional performance; providing cost-effective quality and service to customers that aims at "best in class"; and making the ability to adapt and innovate part of the institutional culture. Given the fast pace of change in today's society, these are important components of long-term financial and academic health for all colleges and universities. Each author speaks from experience about positioning institutions of higher learning for the coming years, using a variety of management and measurement techniques, but all discuss the underlying necessity for change.

Higher education is poised at a critical juncture, one that calls for bold decision-making and new performance standards and measures. Given the major external changes that are being thrust on higher education, it must respond with equal force. Transformation of the way higher education is organized and managed may be in order.

A quote from Peter Drucker found in a recent *Harvard Business Review* article seems an appropriate conclusion to this introduction. According to Drucker's article "The New Society of Organizations," "the modern organization . . . must be organized for the systematic abandonment of whatever is established, customary, familiar, and comfortable, whether that is a product, service, or process; a set of skills; human and social relationships; or the organization itself. In short, it must be organized for constant change."[6]

NOTES

1. Peter F. Drucker, *Managing for the Future: The 1990s and Beyond*, New York: Truman Talley Books/Dutton, 1992, p. 339.

2. Rosabeth Moss Kanter, *When Giants Learn to Dance: Mastering the Challenge of Strategy, Management, and Careers in the 1990s*, New York: Simon and Schuster, 1989, p. 22.

3. Tom Peters, *Thriving on Chaos: Handbook for a Management Revolution*, New York: Alfred A. Knopf, 1987.

4. Ibid., p. 399.

5. Peter F. Drucker, "The New Society of Organizations," *Harvard Business Review*, September-October 1992, p. 97.

6. Ibid., p. 96.

Chapter 1

Measuring Performance in Higher Education

Robert H. Scott

The topic of performance measurement is central to every organization. Without performance measurement we do not know where we are. No matter what course we set, we will never know if we have arrived at the intended destination.

Any intelligent discussion of the measurement of performance requires a clear understanding of the terms. Precisely what is performance? How has it been measured? How can it be measured? How *should* it be measured? What criteria define success and failure? What factors distinguish good performances from bad performances? What actions can or should be taken in response as problems or opportunities are identified? Over what time frames should results be measured?

The establishment of a goal reflects an organizational commitment to change in a specific way or to move in one or more defined directions. While progress toward goals such as those relating to quality, reputation, and contribution to society can be felt more easily than measured, the large majority of the goals established by universities and colleges suggest obvious measures of success. The goal itself may well define the measurement, such as, for example, reducing costs by a specified percentage, increasing the median academic credential for entering students, or reaching a new plateau with respect to alumni fund participation.

There are many different ways in which goals can be set, analyzed, organized, described, and categorized. Some goals are strategic, others are operational. Any organization has, by definition, few strategic goals. However, they are the important ones. Organizational success hinges on selecting strategic goals correctly, on ensuring their compatibility, and on marshaling the resources to achieve them. Strategic goals tend to be enduring. Operational goals, on the other hand, will generally be more specific, more numerous, somewhat transient, and generally easier to measure.

For a business a strategic goal might involve reaching a specified level of return on equity or achievement of a leadership position in one or more markets. For a university a strategic goal might be improving educational and research quality in the sciences, achieving a major change in the demographics of the student body, or gaining a particular level of reputation and recognition.

Goals can also be categorized and analyzed on other dimensions. In higher education some goals will relate to the academic program, while others will address the administrative activities performed or acquired to support the prime objectives of teaching and research. Some goals will be institutionwide, others will be quite department specific. Some goals will be achieved (or not achieved!) in the short term, others will represent truly long-term efforts. In fact, only some goals will be specifically achievable. Others constitute the potentially questionable institutional desire to improve performance no matter how good it already is.

Traditionally, higher education has had difficulty in defining goals clearly, in organizing to achieve them, in measuring performance toward their attainment, and in reporting progress to stakeholders of all types—trustees, faculty, students, alumni, staff, legislators, the media, opinion makers, and the public at large. Over the past decade, however, considerable progress has been made. Today the typical university president can describe institutional goals with ease. More important, institutional goals are being discussed widely within institutions, and institutional leaders are seeking a greater degree of consensus for them because change is more rapid, resources are scarcer, correct choice is more important, and community consensus and support increasingly spell the difference between success and failure.

Why then is it that performance measurement and the reporting of results have seemed so difficult to institutions of higher education? I suggest that there are least two reasons:

- The strategic, academic goals sought by institutions of higher education tend to be somewhat ethereal and elusive of measurement.

- As a consequence, higher education has tended not to think in quantitative terms about its management in general and has not demanded enough of itself in the areas of analysis, operational goal setting, and schedules for progress.

In response to these issues, the past ten years have been filled with discussion about goal setting in higher education. Many institutions have undertaken the development of strategic plans and have worked to position themselves distinctively in various sectors of the education marketplace. The increasing scarcity of resources has made both efficiency and choice more important.

Much of this discussion and many of the consequential actions have been healthy. However, there has been an unavoidable tendency to measure the obvious but perhaps less significant at the expense of the obscure but important. I believe that institutional leadership must focus on the relatively small number of long-term, higher-level goals because these are the issues that are the prerequisites for success and the factors to which leadership can make the most important and unique contribution. Establishment of these goals helps to set the tone, style, and culture for the organization. Lower-level and more detailed goals, which will generally be easier both to achieve and to measure, can and should flow from a clear understanding of the strategic goals.

Setting goals requires several actions, including the following:

- Analysis of the current situation and environment, i.e., an understanding of the market
- Vision to identify and describe all alternatives
- Wisdom to select correctly from alternatives
- Consistency among goals, across the institution, and over time
- Mechanisms for measurement, feedback, and correction

In my experience higher education is performing increasingly well in the process of goal *setting*. As an industry, however, higher education has done less well at *achieving* the goals it sets. In general, we have failed to recognize the importance of continuing management and have tended to leave the achievement of goals to an existing organization, assuming that progress would somehow be made without major administrative effort. Such an approach is often unrealistic. To achieve goals, institutions need:

- An organization appropriately designed for the tasks at hand
- The ability to execute decisions well
- Appropriate levels of communication
- Adequate commitment of executive time

- A determined, long-term focus
- An appropriate level of consistency

Understanding the alternatives, selecting among them, and managing implementation require measurement. Institutions need to:

- Understand the *information* they need and collect the data which provides that information. Information is much more than data: it is that rare indicator which provides insight. However, information must be based on repeatable, correct, and widely understood data.
- Avoid overkill and overload by asking and answering such questions as: Will this information make a difference? Will not having it matter much? Will not having it matter at all?
- Pass over the obvious but insignificant to focus on the important but obscure. By deciding *in advance* what will be the measures of success and failure, institutions can avoid the tendency to self-delusion associated with defining as success that which is about to be achieved. By determining in advance what *might* go wrong, much trouble is avoidable.

Information to support decision making and management of the data on which decision making is based comes from a variety of computer-based, manual, and human systems. Almost all managers use first—and often only—that information which is readily available. This approach is usually suboptimal. Managers need to define specifically the information they need to monitor performance and support choices and then arrange affairs so that this is the information they receive and use.

Management information systems should identify and select for institutional leadership that relatively small number of indicators that are important to strategic planning from among the very large number of administrative indicators that are potentially useful in operations.

All institutions of higher education, and large research universities in particular, are complex entities. However, even for such complex entities there are relatively few facts and indicators about programmatic, financial, and human performance that are central to setting goals and understanding progress. Defining these key variables, monitoring them, and influencing them is a central task of management.

Let me now illustrate these points using two examples taken from my own institution, Harvard University. The first seeks to elucidate both the problem of obtaining the information needed for strategic decisions and the importance of continuity over time; the second addresses an operational problem for which continuous monitoring and change are needed.

- Did we have a good financial year?
- Is our financial aid strategy working?

DID WE HAVE A GOOD FINANCIAL YEAR?

Much has been written about the difficulty of understanding university financial statements. Particularly for those most familiar with the financial affairs of business organizations, university financial reports, which are based on fund accounting, appear difficult to understand at best and incomprehensible at worst. Since university reports provide much information at a disaggregated level, they make it difficult to identify and focus on critical, institutionwide factors.

In the early 1980s Harvard identified this issue as a strategically important factor. We realized that we needed to be able to explain our affairs more clearly to our supporters, and equally important, we knew that we needed to have and use financial reports that demonstrated credibly the degree of progress toward our financial goals. To address these issues, we began a program of analysis in the early 1980s. We identified three major problems:

- The financial statements needed to be changed in order to make them more useful to readers.
- The true cost to the university of facilities, particularly on an inflation-adjusted basis, was neither accurately nor adequately represented in our financial statements.
- Despite the fact that we were reporting "balanced budgets," significant financial liabilities had not been addressed.

As reported in the Harvard University Financial Report for Fiscal 1981-82, we began by preparing pro forma financial reports for selected units of the university using a range of different assumptions. Table 1 presents financial statements for four years for Harvard's School of Public Health using normal university fund-accounting principles and actual data for the period 1979-82. This table shows that the results from operations had turned from a small deficit in the first two years to a small surplus in the second two, that the volume of activity was growing rapidly, and that finan-

Table 1.
Harvard School of Public Health
Comparative Financial Statements 1979–1982

As Reported
(in millions of dollars)

	Beginning Balance	1979	1980	1981	1982
BALANCE SHEET					
Assets:					
Current funds	$ 2.3	$ 1.9	$ 1.1	$ 1.5	$ 2.1
Investments at market value	45.0	48.3	53.5	56.9	52.5
Total	47.3	50.2	54.6	58.4	54.6
Liabilities:					
Debt	.0	.4	.3	.6	.5
Equity, primarily endowment	47.3	49.8	54.3	57.8	54.1
Total	47.3	50.2	54.6	58.4	54.6
OPERATIONS					
Income:					
Endowment income used		2.5	2.7	3.2	3.8
Current gifts used		5.8	7.0	7.0	8.5
Tuition and other student income		1.6	1.7	1.9	2.1
Government grants and contracts		12.1	13.9	17.0	18.5
Other income		.4	.3	.6	.1
Total		22.4	25.6	29.7	33.0
Expense		(22.8)	(26.1)	(29.4)	(32.7)
Results from operations		(.4)	(.5)	.3	.4
Holding gain or (loss) on investments		1.7	3.5	1.2	(4.8)
Addition to or (use) from operations		(.3)	(.2)	(.1)	.4
Net Source or (use) from operations		1.0	2.8	1.4	(4.0)
Gifts and other changes to capital		1.5	1.7	2.1	.3
Increase in equity		2.5	4.5	3.5	(3.7)
EQUITY AT BEGINNING OF YEAR		47.3	49.8	54.3	57.8
EQUITY AT END OF YEAR		$ 49.8	$ 54.3	$ 57.8	$ 54.1

Table 2.
Harvard School of Public Health
Comparative Financial Statements 1979–1982

With Plant and Inflation but in Current Dollars
(in millions of dollars)

	Beginning Balance	1979	1980	1981	1982
BALANCE SHEET					
Assets:					
Current funds	$ 2.3	$ 1.9	$ 1.1	$ 1.5	$ 2.1
Buildings at replacement cost	17.3	18.6	20.1	22.0	23.6
Investments at market value	45.0	48.3	53.5	56.9	52.5
Total	64.6	68.8	74.7	80.4	78.2
Liabilities:					
Debt	.0	.4	.3	.6	.5
Renovation reserve	3.9	4.7	5.5	6.6	7.8
Equity, primarily endowment	60.7	63.7	68.9	73.2	69.9
Total	64.6	68.8	74.7	80.4	78.2
OPERATIONS					
Income:					
Endowment income used		2.5	2.7	3.2	3.8
Current gifts used		5.8	7.0	7.0	8.5
Tuition and other student income		1.6	1.7	1.9	2.1
Government grants and contracts		12.1	13.9	17.0	18.5
Other income		.4	.3	.6	.1
Total		22.4	25.6	29.7	33.0
Expense		(22.8)	(26.1)	(29.4)	(32.6)
Results from operations		(.4)	(.5)	.3	.4
Provision for renovation reserve		(.8)	(.8)	(1.0)	(1.2)
Holding gain or (loss) on investments		1.7	3.5	1.2	(4.8)
Monetary gain or (loss) on investments		(5.0)	(6.9)	(5.1)	(4.0)
Holding and monetary gain or (loss) on buildings and reserve		.0	(.6)	.5	.5
Monetary gain or (loss) on working capital		(.3)	(.2)	(.1)	(.1)
Addition to or (use) from operations		(.3)	(.2)	(.1)	.4
Net Source or (use) from operations		(5.1)	(5.7)	(4.3)	(8.8)
Gifts and other changes to capital		1.5	1.7	2.1	.3
Increase in equity		(3.6)	(4.0)	(2.2)	(8.5)
EQUITY AT BEGINNING OF YEAR		67.3	72.9	75.4	78.4
EQUITY AT END OF YEAR		$ 63.7	$ 68.9	$ 73.2	$ 69.9

Table 3.
Harvard School of Public Health
Comparative Financial Statements 1979–1982

With Plant and Inflation and in Constant 1982 Dollars
(in millions of dollars)

	Beginning Balance	1979	1980	1981	1982
BALANCE SHEET					
Assets:					
Current funds	$ 3.4	$ 2.5	$ 1.3	$ 1.6	$ 2.1
Buildings at replacement cost	25.6	25.0	23.5	23.5	23.6
Investments at market value	67.0	64.8	62.9	61.0	52.5
Total	96.0	92.3	87.7	86.1	78.2
Liabilities:					
Debt	.0	.5	.4	.6	.5
Renovation reserve	5.8	6.3	6.5	7.1	7.8
Equity, primarily endowment	90.2	85.5	80.8	78.4	69.9
Total	96.0	92.3	87.7	80.4	78.2
OPERATIONS					
Income:					
Endowment income used		3.3	3.2	3.4	3.8
Current gifts used		7.8	8.2	7.5	8.5
Tuition and other student income		2.2	2.0	2.0	2.1
Government grants and contracts		16.2	16.3	18.2	18.5
Other income		.5	.4	.6	.1
Total		30.0	25.6	31.7	33.0
Expense		(30.5)	(30.6)	(31.4)	(32.6)
Results from operations		(.5)	(.5)	.3	.4
Provision for renovation reserve		(1.1)	(1.0)	(1.2)	(1.2)
Holding gain or (loss) on investments.		2.3	4.1	1.3	(4.8)
Monetary gain or (loss) on investments		(6.6)	(8.1)	(5.5)	(4.0)
Monetary gain or (loss) on buildings ..		.0	(.7)	.6	.5
Monetary gain or (loss) on working capital		(.3)	(.2)	(.1)	(.1)
Addition to or (use) from operations...		(.5)	(.3)	(.1)	.4
Net Source or (use) from operations.		(6.7)	(6.7)	(4.7)	(8.8)
Gifts and other changes to capital		2.0	2.0	2.3	.3
Increase in equity		(4.7)	(4.7)	(2.4)	(8.5)
EQUITY AT BEGINNING OF YEAR .		90.2	85.5	80.8	78.4
EQUITY AT END OF YEAR		$ 85.5	$ 80.8	$ 78.4	$ 69.9

Table 4.
Harvard School of Public Health
Comparative Financial Statements 1979–1982

Summaries of Effects of Different Accounting Methods
(in millions of dollars)

	1979	1980	1981	1982	Cumulative
SCHOOL OF PUBLIC HEALTH					
Increase (decrease) in equity:					
As reported	$ 2.5	$ 4.5	$ 3.5	$ (3.7)	$ 6.8
With plant and inflation					
1982 constant dollars	(4.7)	(4.7)	(2.4)	(8.5)	(20.3)
DIVINITY SCHOOL					
Increase (decrease) in equity:					
As reported	1.5	2.4	1.5	(1.6)	3.8
With plant and inflation					
1982 constant dollars	(1.9)	(2.1)	(1.5)	(3.8)	(9.3)
BUSINESS SCHOOL					
Increase (decrease) in equity:					
As reported	10.8	16.4	15.1	2.1	44.4
With plant and inflation					
1982 constant dollars	0.2	(0.8)	3.6	(5.7)	(2.7)

cial equity was growing to match. Is this an accurate representation of the affairs of this school? We suspected not.

Table 2 shows these same data with adjustments to reflect a provision for the renovation of facilities sufficient to charge to the years in question the value of plant consumed during those years. In addition, these statements are adjusted to reflect the effect of rising prices. Instead of showing small average increases in equity, the statements show rather significant decreases. Since these decreases were approximately matched by national inflation, equity appears stable. Does this represent the situation reasonably? Again, we suspected not.

Table 3 shows the same data but with a further adjustment to use 1982 dollars throughout. This report shows that the budget of the School of Public Health was growing only slowly and that the School was consuming—not building—its equity. This statement is a far more accurate and useful description of the school's affairs.

The application of this analysis to three quite different Harvard schools is summarized in Table 4. These analyses showed Harvard the importance of reflecting plant on the balance sheet and of considering inflation. They had a significant effect on our future activities.

After completing this exercise, we developed the following working definition of an answer to the question "Did you have a good financial year?"

> We had a good year if, with all expenses accrued and after inflation, net assets have grown sufficiently to support actual and planned program improvements.

We then set two related goals:

- Develop a systematic program for estimating and meeting university needs for plant renewal and build the resources to achieve those improvements into the annual budget
- Modify the financial statements to improve their comprehensiveness and clarity

Achieving the first objective has involved many people at Harvard. Financial models were constructed and tested, buildings were surveyed and measured, renovation backlogs were estimated, major programs for renovation were undertaken, and budgets were adjusted, over a period of years, to make adequate provision for renovation. To achieve the second objective, numerous discussions were held with users of our financial reports: trustees, administrators, alumni, selected faculty at Harvard and elsewhere, investment bankers, bond-rating agencies, the accounting community, and so forth. As a consequence, the format for our financial statements was changed to provide reports that came as close to meeting the university's needs as was possible within the framework of generally accepted accounting principles for universities and in recognition of the direction in which those principles are developing.

Over the decade of the 1980s approximately half of the annual need for maintenance was built into the university's operating budget. In 1991 our financial statements were changed to the new format. That change received considerable discussion within higher education during 1992. During the 1990s Harvard plans to build into its budget the remaining funds needed to maintain plant, so that by the year 2000, when we say that we have a "balanced budget," we will be reflecting all costs. In addition, and as further modification to accounting principles governing universities are considered, we plan to play a major role in encouraging the evolution and adop-

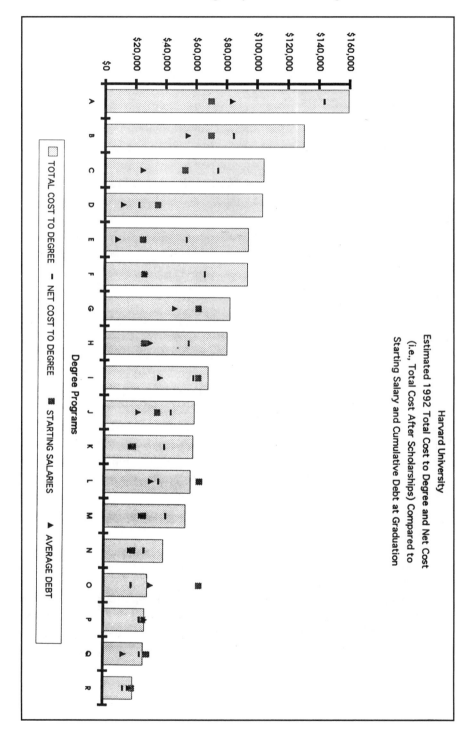

Harvard University
Estimated 1992 Total Cost to Degree and Net Cost
(i.e., Total Cost After Scholarships) Compared to
Starting Salary and Cumulative Debt at Graduation

tion of standards that make university accounting more like that for the business enterprises with which we are all compared with increasing frequency.

IS OUR FINANCIAL AID STRATEGY WORKING?

At different institutions and at different times, financial aid meets different objectives. At some institutions it serves to fill places; at others it fosters institutional objectives by attracting the most desirable students. For the nation as a whole financial aid meets the important social policy of making higher education (public or private) accessible to all. For many students and their families financial aid also provides a vehicle for financing a large capital cost and for spreading that cost over a number of years.

What criteria should be employed? When should financial aid be provided as a scholarship and when as a loan? When is financial aid a "financing" and when is it a "gift"? Are student debt loads too burdensome? To provide and communicate relevant data about these interrelated choices, Harvard designed Chart 1, which identifies key controllable variables and presents data in a relatively simple form. Four factors are involved: the cost of a degree (i.e., total student budget for one year multiplied by the number of years to complete the degree), the net cost to the student (i.e., the gross cost of a degree less scholarship aid), the student's starting salary at graduation, and the student's debt level at graduation.

Some desirable relationships between these factors are self-evident. Higher starting salaries will support higher debt loads. Larger scholarships are needed where starting salaries are lower, where annual educational costs are higher, and where programs are longer. Better scholarship programs may attract superior students; however, such a strategy requires larger levels of expenditure. Other relationships are less obvious. To what extent should aid be related to need and cost, and to what extent should long-term increases in earning capacity be reflected? How much program-to-program difference in the level of student aid and expected family contributions should be tolerated?

Obviously, this chart can be used both to describe the current situation and to permit consideration of various possible alternatives. A computer model underlying the chart permits Harvard to examine the consequences of possible changes to policy in ways that are fully useful and comprehensible to both experts and generalists alike.

* * *

These two examples seek to illustrate my main points. When important goals are set, adequate plans must be made to measure performance toward their achievement. Such measurement is not only necessary for progress; it should be an integral part of the goal-setting process. By establishing good benchmarks, by communicating the importance of achieving them, by focusing effort on their attainment, by maintaining that focus for an adequate period of time, by determining what information is needed to support management, and by acquiring and using that information, much can be accomplished.

Chapter 2

Measuring Performance: How Colleges and Universities Can Set Meaningful Goals and Be Accountable

William F. Massy

The headline for a recent article in *The Economist* opened with this encouraging thought: "Academia is the one bit of education in which America still leads the world." Then it dropped the other shoe: "But for how much longer?"[1]

According to *The Economist*, and a great many contemporary critics of U.S. higher education, colleges' and universities' costs are too high, and their ability to deliver value for money is problematic. In addition to the well-known problem of labor intensity, the high costs are due to a faculty labor market that is out of control, soaring research expense, and the fact that internal and external constituencies expect—and demand—that their institutions be all things to all people. The result is dwindling affordability, erosion of faculty accountability, and proliferation of programs and ideologies to the point where the general public has begun to question the whole enterprise. No wonder a populist backlash threatens deeply held academic values and leaves many academics with feelings of bewilderment and anger.

These problems will not go away. The affordability crunch is rooted in long-term pressures on the standard of living for the middle class: because of the diffusion of productive capacity around the world, and the resulting increase of international competition, today's young people can no longer look forward to automatic real income enhancements. A global tide of "deprotectionism," withdrawal of special privilege in both the social and economic spheres, fuels resentment over perceived faculty life-styles, perquisites, and freedom from accountability. Fragmentation of values in the larger society and the rise of in-your-face activism reinforce program proliferation on the one hand and popular resentment about particular programs and ideologies on the other. These forces are too strong—and too rooted in real ills—for the problem to be simply ridden out or assuaged by rhetorical and political defenses.

Colleges and universities must change their behavior. They must become more productive. They must learn to set meaningful goals and be accountable for achieving them

A PROGRAM FOR ACCOUNTABILITY

There is nothing particularly mysterious about accountability, even in higher education. The Presidential Commission on the Responsibility for Financing Higher Education put forward this four-point program:

1. Decide on the tasks that need to be accomplished, i.e., the goals of the enterprise.
2. Ensure that the available resources are sufficient to complete the tasks successfully.
3. Provide the enterprise with the authority it needs to be effective, and then let it do the job without interference.
4. Define a set of measurements to indicate how well the enterprise is doing relative to its goals, and follow up by tracking these measurements.[2]

These principles apply at every level of the accountability stream: in higher education, the stream runs from state governments (for public institutions) to governing boards, to system and campus administrations, to academic units like schools and departments, and finally to individual faculty. No level should be exempt, but no level should feel disempowered either. Decisions about goals should be participatory, for example, although the authority for goal-setting must ultimately reside with those who provide funds and are held accountable by others for their use. (This authority locus is mandated by the third principle, applied one level up the chain.) Assessment of resource sufficiency and the design of measurements also should be participative, since the downstream units know more about productivity methods and measures than the upstream ones. Once again, however, the upstream unit needs to stay close enough to the action to be sure that the assessments and measures are reasonable. Finally, the local unit's authority to act autonomously to achieve the agreed goals provides the ultimate empowerment needed to motivate and enable the needed productive capacity.

Apologists for higher education will argue that accountability is inappropriate because only academicians know what is good in education and research, and because it is impossible to measure success in achieving the "good." We must reject that way of thinking. The first proposition is false on its face, since funds are spent on education and research in order to achieve certain educational and social objectives—which in turn must be traded off against other goods. Like medicine, higher education has become too large and costly to warrant delegation of goals and resource needs to the self-interested professionals within the enterprise. (This is one of the tenets of deprotectionism.) The second proposition is false as well, as I shall demonstrate in the remainder of this paper.

PRESTIGE AS GOAL AND PROBLEM

The criticism of colleges and universities does not arise from an inability to define goals and measure performance, but rather because too many institutions have defined the wrong goal and have been all too effective in measuring progress toward achieving it. According to Harvard emeritus president Derek Bok:

> As we all know, the prizes, the media recognition, the extra income do not come from working with students or engaging in exemplary teaching. And it is not just the professors' incentives that are out of whack, but also those of administrators. What presidents and deans are held accountable for is improving the prestige of their institutions, and the *prestige* of their institutions comes from the research reputation of their faculties.[3]

Put in the best light, prestige has come to be viewed as a surrogate for higher education's contribution to society. Research is a "good" because it opens the way for new solutions and opportunities, and the prizes, media recognition, and extra income simply reflect its value. Prestige brings the institution comparative advantage in the competitive market for faculty as well as intrinsic pride in accomplishment and recognition. Successful prestige-building reinforces the importance of research (and its close cousin, graduate education), and failure brings both tangible and intangible penalties. Institutions compete for prestige, and over time the quest becomes self-fulfilling and regenerating.

Figure 1.
The Tradeoff between Educational Quality and Research

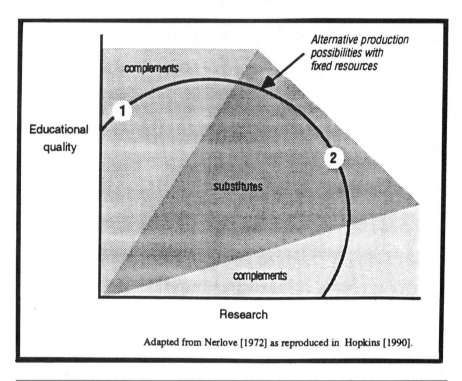

Adapted from Nerlove [1972] as reproduced in Hopkins [1990].

While there is nothing wrong with prestige-building per se, an expanding body of opinion holds that the process has gone too far and that many of higher education's ills can be attributed to this fact. Unbridled competition for prestige—at least as traditionally defined in terms of research—leads to "mission creep," as evidenced by the drive of many institutions to become "universities." It increases cost per student as the "academic ratchet" adds to institutionally funded faculty discretionary time, which in turn is deployed to produce yet more research and scholarship.[4] It overwhelms researchers and libraries with exponentially growing volumes of research output—much of dubious quality—often promulgated in journals created more to meet faculty needs for publication than to disseminate information demanded by readers. It puts a "whatever-it-takes" premium on the recruitment and retention of faculty research stars and places promising young educators who do not excel at research in counterproductive "publish or perish" situations. It adds to the proliferation of support services as more tasks are offloaded from faculty. Finally, it deprives undergraduate and professional students of faculty "quality time" that otherwise could be used for the modernization of educational goals, the design of new curricula and teaching methods, and teaching itself.

These problems are not unique to research universities. To quote Carnegie Foundation for the Advancement of Teaching President Ernie Boyer:

> The pressure to publish, while found to one degree or another in all types of institutions in our study, was especially apparent at those universities or doctorate-granting institutions that see themselves as "being in transition." The goal, as an administrator at one such institution put it, is "to be in the top twenty, or certainly in the top fifty." Meanwhile, the same institutions enroll large numbers of undergraduates, and members of the faculty—especially young faculty members—often feel caught in the middle.[5]
>
> Small liberal arts colleges may have a culture of their own. Faculty may teach more and spend more time with their students. But even these institutions live in the shadow of the research university. They value good teaching but are likely to reward most handsomely those members of the faculty who have scholarly reputations. A paper read at a national convention nets more praise than a splendid lecture to undergraduates. A published article in a prestigious journal or a major book is valued most of all.[6]

Defenders of research's primacy among institutional goals argue that research excellence is a necessary condition for excellence in teaching, and that by maximizing research (and its surrogate, prestige) the benefits conferred on undergraduates also will be maximized. For many institutions this was the original justification for upgrading research. The assertion is correct up to a certain point, especially if the definition of research is broadened to include general scholarship and keeping up with one's field. However, the process has gone too far in a growing number of institutions, to the point where research substitutes for education to an alarming degree. Worse yet, too many institutions strive to emulate this overcommitment to research.

Figure 1 depicts the various combinations of educational quality and research that could be produced by a hypothetical academic unit, given that faculty and other resource levels are fixed.[7] (I consider the quantity of education as fixed for purposes of the illustration but make no distinction between the quantity and quality of research.) Research and education are *complements in production* up to a certain point, as depicted in the figure's first gray triangle. At the low research levels depicted by point 1, increments to research improve educational quality for the traditional reasons of intellectual currency and excitement. However, successive increments to research bring diminishing returns. The conventional wisdom holds that the emphasis on research is about right or perhaps even too low. However, as research is pushed further the time demands on faculty and support staff take their toll. Educational quality and research become *substitutes* as one passes into the figure's second gray triangle. The research environment is competitive and open-ended, so the pressure on research time never lets up. Hence the amount of effort devoted to teaching must increase disproportionately as one moves downward toward point 2. While not relevant to the present discussion, it is worth noting that research and education become complements again at low levels of educational output, for example, in pure research institutes that do not benefit from the students' paradigm-breaking questions and inexpensive research labor.

Outside funding may reduce teaching loads and allow extra faculty to be hired, but it also brings new tasks such as proposal-writing and meeting sponsor-imposed deadlines. Faculty with significant research programs shift their allegiance from the institution outward toward their discipline and sponsors, breaking down the academic work-unit's sense of community. I am convinced that on balance, the cross-pressures generated by sponsored research programs put more pressure on undergraduate teaching performance than the extra funding alleviates through contributions to the institution's fixed cost. Higher education's critics believe with some justification that too many institutions have moved well into the substitutability region—where increments to research crowd out quality teaching time.

But maximizing prestige can lead to even more pernicious consequences than missing the optimal point in the difficult tradeoff between research and educational quality. It can undermine financial discipline and end up exploiting the institution's future stakeholders, as well as current undergraduates, to benefit today's faculty and administrators. Calls for deficit spending in hard economic times to avoid degrading faculty morale are all too familiar. Losing prestigious faculty members erodes prestige to an extent disproportionate to the effect on educational quality. No institutional leader wants the responsibility (or the accountability) for such losses; many will go to extraordinary lengths to avoid them, regardless of the long-term consequences. These pressures also distort facilities maintenance decisions, transfers to capital budgets, and endowment payout rates.

Performance-measure asymmetry biases decisions away from educational quality and increases cost. Research accomplishment tends to be easier to measure than educational accomplishment—the work product is tangible and can be subjected to peer review, and it does not depend so much on the quality and motivation of the "raw material." Furthermore, faculty research productivity can be transferred more easily from institution to institution than can educational productivity. (The latter depends more on school-specific characteristics like curriculum, student attributes, and culture.) Hence the research marketplace has become very competitive, whereas the educational marketplace remains quite imperfect. Competition bids up the price of the research stars, as manifested in compensation, reduced teaching loads, and better support services and facilities. Institutions must appropriate an ever-larger fraction of their resources—including those intended for undergraduate and professional education—to sustain or improve their standing in the faculty marketplace.

Higher education's leaders and faculty did not set out to charge more for undergraduate education while providing less. Originally, the goal was to increase instructional quality by moving up the ascending portion of the curve in Figure 1. But, lacking explicit goal definitions, performance measures, and accountability for undergraduate educational quality and cost-effectiveness, the "researchification" process has encountered no natural stopping point. It has proceeded to ratchet along under its own power, producing these consequences:

- less time devoted to undergraduate and professional education
- less concern about the structure and coherence of the curriculum
- larger budgets and higher tuition
- greater pressure to transfer resources from future to present stakeholders

The juxtaposition of these consequences worries students, parents, donors, state and federal officials, and others who fund undergraduate and professional education.

Table 1.
Approaches to Institutional Performance Improvement

	Educational tasks	*Administrative and support tasks*
	I	II
Do the right things	Develop new faculty incentives	Design appropriate services, incentives, and management systems
	Restore the balance between teaching and research, and design a more effective curriculum	
	III	IV
Do things right	Deliver effective teaching and advising	Insure effective program implementation
	Control costs	Control costs
	V	
Maintain financial discipline	Allocate resources effectively Maintain financial equilibrium	

The conclusion is simple and inescapable. To regain the public trust, colleges and universities must redefine their goals to emphasize more than prestige and its main driver, faculty research. The new goals must focus on the needs of the undergraduate and professional clients whose education represents the primary mission for most institutions and the objectives of those who provide the funding for them. While research should continue to be important, accountability requires that institutions demonstrate a reasonable balance between the resources dedicated to research and those used for education. This, in turn, requires that colleges and universities develop new success measures, that the media and other opinion leaders start publicizing and using them, and that institutional stakeholders accept the broader measures—and the goals from which they are derived—as a valid basis for accountability. Higher education should heed *The Economist*'s final dictum: "For once, a little more introspection on the part of the academic community seems to be in order."[8]

IMPROVING INSTITUTIONAL PERFORMANCE

To restore the public trust, academia's new introspection will have to improve the quality and cost-effectiveness of undergraduate education and demonstrate value for money. Table 1 outlines the dimensions of the task. The horizontal dimension divides the institution along academic and nonacademic lines, the vertical dimension articulates two classic quality-efficiency questions[9] plus the need to maintain financial discipline, and the cells contain examples of the kinds of tasks that need to be accomplished.[10] I shall focus here on cells I and III, plus the cost-control element of cell IV. I also have been working on issues pertaining to cell V.[11] Cells II and IV have been addressed elsewhere.[12]

Restoring the balance between teaching and research does not mean turning back the clock to the preresearch era, nor does it mean turning faculty into high-volume teaching machines. To attempt either would be to throw away an important element of college and university competence; indeed, it would negate the comparative advantage of the tertiary education sector. We need better balance, not a new overreaction that takes us back to the northwest corner of Figure 1.

Controlling costs and maintaining financial discipline need not diminish quality. Cost control means doing things efficiently, and more effective resource allocation can concentrate money where it can make the biggest difference. By maintaining financial equilibrium, institutional leaders can avoid overspending endowment and reserve funds and building liabilities for their successors—the two classic methods for exploiting future stakeholders. Successful businesses have learned that a good restructuring program can improve quality *and* reduce cost, and we should aspire to do no less in higher education.

Educational quality is like industrial quality in another very important respect: it must be built in from the beginning, it cannot be "inspected in" afterwards. Effective service providers put the client first during the design phase, insist on total dedication to client needs during the service encounter, and then obtain and carefully analyze feedback from clients to maintain a process of continuous improvement. In higher education this means designing a meaningful curriculum, delivering effective teaching, carefully monitoring results, and making continuous adjustments to curriculum and teaching methods in response to client feedback and new technological opportunities. Such a program is not incompatible with striving for excellence in research and scholarship, but it will require a change in culture at many institutions.

Businesses have learned that the best way to achieve quality is to provide clear goals and appropriate resources, decentralize to self-directed work teams, and insist on effective performance feedback. (It is no accident that these stand in one-to-one correspondence with the four necessary conditions for accountability.) Higher education has gotten the formula partly right: over the last forty years we have marshaled the resources needed to do an effective job of education, and we have given institutions and their faculty the independence needed to do the job. We even began with a clear vision: that by upgrading research we would, ipso facto, improve educational quality. Unfortunately, however, our vision was not clear enough to foresee the consequences of carrying research to an extreme or to predict that combining ample resources and heavy decentralization with fuzzy educational goals and one-sided performance measures would unleash the prestige-maximization monster.

Colleges and universities should reflect on their mission and its implications for the education-research balance, redefine undergraduate education in terms of client need and value for money, redouble their efforts to maintain financial discipline, and develop appropriate performance measures. The objective should be significant quality improvements and cost reductions in areas not essential to the central academic mission—in other words, institutional restructuring.

RESTRUCTURING TASKS AND PERFORMANCE MEASURES

Restructuring requires the design and implementation of specific programs—high-sounding generalities won't do. The requirements follow the four-point program for accountability described earlier; however, restructuring necessitates a richer mixture of leadership, incentives, motivation, and assistance than does simple accountability. The following recommendations apply to both the academic and nonacademic sectors in all kinds of colleges and universities.

1. *Vision*: develop a clear vision for the changes that need to be accomplished and why they are important. Success becomes more likely when people understand clearly what is desired and why they should change their habitual ways of thinking and behaving. It should go without saying that institutional leaders must be strongly and visibly committed to the vision and demonstrate that commitment by actions as well as words.

2. *Resources*: ensure that needed resources are available in a timely and nonbureaucratic way. Investments in new equipment and technical assistance can be important for their own sake and also because they demonstrate commitment to the restructuring program and trust in the teams that drive it. Nothing will kill restructuring faster than achieving buy-in on the vision and then stifling initiatives with bureaucratic approval processes and "can't-do" managerial attitudes.

3. *Autonomy*: provide employee groups with (a) the autonomy they need to identify and implement the specific changes needed for restructuring, and (b) clear statements about goals and limits, plus meaningful incentives based on the goals. In academic units the faculty already are largely self-directed, but too many fail to focus sufficiently on education, and there is too much fragmentation for effective teamwork.[13] The emphasis in academic work units should be on goals, limits, and incentives rather than autonomy per se; however, one should not try to micromanage faculty time.

4. *Performance measures*: agree on performance measures for each restructuring task, and then follow up to ensure that work groups are paying attention to the measures. Performance measures should represent aids to self-directed work improvement, not something unilaterally imposed and monitored by "the boss." While those with upstream accountability must track downstream performance and frequently discuss it with the responsible work teams, the relationship should be "win-win" rather than "gotcha."

Performance measures should focus on process and inputs as well as output assessment. For example, the way a work group approaches its task sometimes can be a good predictor of effectiveness: certain kinds of processes increase the probability of success, while others may virtually preclude it. Observing the input to a process will be important when time-on-task is problematic—as it is in the case for teaching-related activities, for example. This does not mean installing time clocks; it does mean learning to ask probing questions about priorities and time allocations.

The tendency for institutions and the press to use expense per student as a quality surrogate has produced some well-justified criticism about input and process measures as predictors of quality. I do not wish to argue against measuring output quality and cost-effectiveness whenever and wherever one can. On the other hand, the difficulty of measuring higher-education output quality means we will have to rely heavily on input and process measures for the foreseeable future. Furthermore, a closer look at the facts behind the criticisms reveals that much of the so-called "expense per student" does not get applied to education at all but rather to faculty research and unneeded administrative and support services. A true accounting probably would indicate a better correlation between education input levels and output quality.

The mutually reinforcing character of output, process, and input measures becomes more apparent when we look at the cascading relationship among workplace processes. The outputs of certain processes become inputs to others, forming a complex network of dependence relationships. (This is one reason why flow-charting is included in so many industrial work-team training programs.) Examining the quantity and quality of inputs needed for one process informs output-specification writing for other processes. My experience indicates that it doesn't make much difference whether one starts by looking at inputs, processes, or outputs—all will have to be confronted sooner or later. Indeed, the categories tend to run together in academic work units, as we will see in the examples presented later.

Performance-measure design should be addressed in a practical, not a strictly "scientific" way. Social scientists tend to approach higher-education outcomes assessment too rigorously, for example, by trying to solve a narrow slice of the problem according to the standards of scientific proof or else throwing up their hands because the whole problem refuses to yield to such standards. Managers in business and government organizations know that one has to take a "what seems right, what seems to work" point of view. This does not mean that scientific method and insight should be cast aside—there is, after all, nothing so practical as a good theory. One should carry rigorous research as far as possible, but be prepared to make leaps of commitment to imperfect but implementable measures that offer a reasonable promise of improving the status quo.

The performance-measure design problem can be addressed by asking two different kinds of questions.

1. "If I were a hands-on work-team member, what would I need in order to track and improve my performance?" For example, how might professors gain better insight into how well their teaching is "going over" and how well the curriculum meets the needs of nontraditional students? How might support service customers gauge the quality of the outputs they receive and provide feedback to the suppliers so that their own performance can be improved?

2. "How do the cost and quality of particular final and intermediate outputs compare with roughly similar outputs provided by other institutions?" What kinds of unit-cost comparisons would be most useful? How could reasonably common definitions be assured, and how should the set of "roughly similar" institutions be defined? Should one base the comparisons on "best practice" in a given institutional segment—on the grounds that one should aspire to be the best—or on a measure of central tendency?

The first type of question digs deeply into one's own organization. The second seeks more aggregate comparisons among a group of peer institutions. In-house information may be obtained by consultants, but the most effective source is the membership of the work units themselves. Comparability data, usually called "benchmark data," often are developed by consortia of institutions or by commercial suppliers. A hybrid, known as "best-practice benchmarking," has been popularized in connection with the Malcomb Baldridge business quality awards: the "best" firm at performing a given function is identified and its methods used as a model for others.

PERFORMANCE MEASURES FOR TEACHING QUALITY

The preceding discussion was necessarily rather abstract, so I will illustrate what I have in mind by means of examples, beginning with the issue of educational quality as it applies to question 1. The broad subject of outcomes assessment is beyond the scope of this paper. However, I hope to show that defining and measuring performance is not as difficult as the conventional wisdom suggests, and that meaningful progress is possible.

It is difficult to achieve consensus on a comprehensive definition of teaching, yet most people believe they "know it when they see it." The following statement by the Committee on Inquiry of England's Polytechnics & Colleges Funding Council (now merged into the Higher Education Funding Council) captures the essence of good teaching:

> The Committee agreed that teaching must be interpreted broadly, as the initiation and management of student learning by a teacher; we also agreed that it must be responsive to student needs; and the conditions necessary for good teaching must be a priority at every level of the institution. We did not identify one definition of "good" teaching, but rather agreed that teaching must be judged good by whether it contributes to the purposes of higher education—the life-chances of the student. However, we also agreed that for excellence in teaching, it was vital to look to the ethos of the institution as a whole, to the sense of excitement amongst students, teachers, and visitors.[14]

The definition delineates the behavior we wish to encourage in order to improve teaching: in this case whether the teacher manages the learning process (as opposed to being passive or reactive), and whether responsiveness to student needs is a priority at every institutional level. The need to determine whether these behavior patterns are being achieved provides the basis for a first round of performance-measure design.

Analyzing the desired behavior in detail provides material for designing a richer set of measures. Teaching is, in effect, the delivery of a service, and the behaviors needed for effective service delivery also are necessary for effective teaching. Research on service delivery shows that two conditions are required to achieve excellence:

1. The provider must care about the client, engaging fully in the task and doing his or her best to understand and adapt to the client's needs.

2. The provider must arrange for feedback about the service encounter—from the client, from knowledgeable observers, or both—and then use the feedback to improve performance.

Effective service delivery requires a high degree of attention and caring, and the difficulty of putting oneself in the client's shoes' requires systematic feedback and conscious adaptation. The need for feedback does not imply that a professional service provider must abdicate to the client's whims; it is up to the professional to apply his or her expertise in the client's service. The client also has a duty: students, for example, should strive to learn. However, the teachers' greater expertise makes them the "team captains" of the learning process. Input-type performance measures can assess the captains' commitment and attention, and process-type measures can assess the feedback arrangements.

The need for redefining the faculty "equity ethic" to encompass the principle of comparative advantage offers additional possibilities for performance-measure design. Though almost anyone can improve his or her performance through sustained effort, all professors do not have the same innate talents. Every institution's faculty can be arrayed according to relative ability in teaching and research. Some professors are outstanding in both—the "stars" that every school seeks to recruit and retain. Some turn out to have more research talent than teaching talent, and for some the balance will be reversed. Ideally only a few—mistakes in selection and promotion—turn out to lack sustainable ability in either research or teaching. An effective program for improving teaching quality would encourage professors who turn out better at teaching than research to focus their attention on teaching and be rewarded for so doing. This application of the comparative advantage principle is frustrated by the low status of teaching in many institutions. Improving the status of teaching would improve quality and, at the same time, relieve a source of tension for many faculty members. Teaching status is a measurable quantity and an important performance variable.

Good teaching encompasses exemplary classroom performance, but that is not all. The "initiation and management of student learning" begins with the development of a coherent curriculum. It continues with advising students about which curricular options can best meet their individual needs and mentoring them in ways that facilitate learning. Classroom performance also includes packaging and presenting materials in ways that make sense to the kinds of students being taught. For example, nontraditional students and disadvantaged minority students require different approaches than well-prepared traditional students. Finally, learning facilitation must include feedback to students about their performance. The findings from Berkeley professor Patricia Cross's classroom research project support the importance of feedback for students as well as faculty.[15] Once again, characterization of the desired behavior illuminates new possibilities for performance-measure design.

Table 2 lists some of the actions that faculty work-groups and institutions might take to promote good undergraduate teaching. The list is not exhaustive, nor do I suggest that all the actions should be required—mere bureaucratic compliance would not be useful, for instance. Nevertheless, good-faith efforts to improve performance, pursued consistently for a period of years, do seem likely to improve educational quality. The actions are

Table 2.
Actions That Might Be Taken by Faculty Work-Groups and Institutions to Promote Good Teaching

Faculty work-groups

Develop clear goals and objectives related specifically to teaching and to the needs of the different kinds of students.

Develop strategies to make teaching a subject of vibrant discussion in faculty meetings and informal conversations, and to make good teaching a source of individual and collective satisfaction.

Encourage senior faculty to play exemplary teaching roles; shun systematic relief from teaching for senior faculty based on seniority.

Develop and maintain effective programs for (a) instructing doctoral students on effective teaching, (b) inculcating attitudes conducive to good teaching, and (c) providing knowledge about how faculty leaders can stimulate good teaching in their work groups.

Establish and enforce criteria for ensuring that junior faculty demonstrate good teaching as well as good research in order to be eligible for promotion.

Arrange for systematic feedback from students, and evaluation of faculty teaching by peers, in relation to goals.

Relate faculty salary increases to good teaching as well as to research; make sure the unit's best teachers' salaries keep pace with those of the best researchers, despite the latter's greater external visibility.

Work through retreats, resource people, and persuasive communication by senior faculty to develop group norms for continuing professional development of teaching skills by all faculty. Develop incentives

for individual faculty to meet or exceed the group norms.

Regularly assess all aspects of the teaching program in a systematic way (e.g., using ideas presented earlier in this chapter), by self-study and use of external resources.

Institutions

Engage work groups in serious dialogue about their teaching goals and performance; require serious planning for better teaching.

Make sure that work groups develop effective mechanisms for assessing teaching quality on an ongoing basis.

Require periodic departmental self-studies of teaching and arrange for external reviews of departmental performance, including teaching.

Provide resources for professional development of teaching skills, such as teaching and learning centers. Make sure work groups develop appropriate norms and incentives for using these resources.

Reward exemplary teachers with institutional prizes or other forms of recognition.

Adjust the criteria for promotion and tenure review (a) to require demonstration of good teaching and (b) to limit the quantity (but not the quality) of research output considered, to make it possible for junior faculty to invest time in teaching.

Monitor effective teaching loads carefully; prevent unintended upward creep of departmental research.

Relate discretionary budget allocations to work-group performance on all of the above.

within reach of most faculties and institutions, and thoughtful observers can determine how things are going without using special tests or techniques. Each item in the list begins with an action verb, which carries the basis for eventual performance evaluation. The list demonstrates that colleges and universities do not lack ways to assess progress toward educational quality—in fact, there may be an embarrassment of riches.

BENCHMARKS

The myth of incomparability has bedeviled higher education for a long time. Many college and university leaders believe that their institutions possess such unique characteristics that efforts to compare one with another will be self-defeating if not damaging. This can represent a self-fulfilling prophecy: for example, there is little standardization among management information system designs or data element definitions. Despite the guidelines promulgated by NACUBO, the Financial Accounting Standards Board (for private institutions), and the Government Accounting Standards Board (for public institutions), accounting methods remain differentiated to the point where meaningful comparisons are difficult or impossible. Institutional representatives fight standardization efforts tooth and nail, partly because of the expense and disruption associated with change and partly, one suspects, because these efforts challenge the incomparability myth.

Even the well-known OMB circular A-21, on which research overhead recovery has been based for many years, is loaded with escape clauses. The resulting "flexibility" permits institutions to define data their own way—and thus escape comparability even on so basic a quantity as an overhead rate. Some modest recommendations on ways to improve the situation, put forth by the AAU Committee on Indirect Cost Recovery a few years ago,[16] were greeted with strong opposition from institutional accounting and financial officers. I outlined the dangers of incomparability in a 1990 presentation.[17] Ironically, government agencies and the press proceeded to make comparisons anyway—on the basis of fragmentary information and anecdotal evidence—and drew flawed and damaging conclusions.

However understandable its genesis, the incomparability myth has taken on the same coloration as the prestige-maximization monster. That is, higher education's critics are coming to view it as an oversimplification or even as a device to enhance market power. Believers in the oversimplification argument hold that comparability can be improved if one is willing to analyze the situation deeply enough, and that there is no excuse for failing to do so. Careful attention to definition, and systematic data analysis and modeling where applicable, can produce valid comparisons in the financial arena—as Gordon Winston points out, for instance.[18] The same is true even in the difficult area of faculty teaching loads and discretionary time.[19]

The idea that incomparability enhances market power derives from the economic principle that pure competition (the antithesis of incomparability) precludes economic exploitation, whereas incomparability makes every entity a monopolist to some degree. Holding an enterprise accountable for efficiency and quality is difficult without good benchmarks. The market provides the needed benchmark in the competitive situation, but when markets are imperfect (as in the case of educational outputs) or nonexistent (as for many administrative and support services), derived benchmarks must be constructed to achieve comparability.

Benchmark information for colleges and universities can be obtained from a number of sources. The federal government collects aggregate information on a number of variables and distributes them at modest cost via the HEGIS/IPEDS and CASPAR databases. The Higher Education Data Sharing (HEDS) organization collects and disseminates more detailed information for member institutions on a cooperative basis. The Association of Governing Boards of Universities and Colleges (AGB) published a book of strategic indicators last year[20] and has updated and significantly enhanced the collection in a publication produced in collaboration with Peterson's Guides. I will conclude this paper by describing the latter effort, with which Joel Meyerson and I have been closely associated.

To be effective, benchmark data must deal with managerially meaningful variables. Hence the design of benchmark surveys must be guided by an implicit or explicit model delineating the important inputs, processes, and outputs for the type of enterprise in question. It will come as no surprise that my preference is for explicit models, ones that can at least potentially be defined in quantitative terms. Explicit models offer the dual advantages of being (a) relatively unambiguous and (b) capable of assessment in terms of internal consistency and completeness on important issues.[21]

Table 3 presents the categories and selected first-level subcategories used in the Peterson's-AGB survey. The first category, "financial profiles," generally follows the IPEDS format, but we added detail in many categories. For example, the figures for "expenditures by function" include the following breakouts (in addition to an "other" category), which we based on budgeting experience, indirect cost analysis, and production function modeling:

Academic support

- libraries
- academic computing

Institutional support

- government, public, and alumni relations; development
- telecommunications and administrative computing

Student services

- admissions and financial aid administration
- student health

Plant operation and maintenance

- plant and grounds maintenance
- utilities

Additional models informed our specification-writing for the other variables: e.g., models for (a) the interinstitutional comparison of indirect costs,[22] (b) the relation of endowment, plant, and maintenance expenditures to long-run financial equilibrium,[23] and (c) faculty age and tenure distributions.[24] More than seven hundred institutions responded to the survey.

The Peterson's-AGB strategic-indicators survey serves the dual objective of focusing attention on important strategic quantities and providing benchmarks for performance assessment. To our knowledge, this is the most comprehensive effort of its kind ever undertaken in higher education. Current plans are to replicate the survey approximately every two years, so that data series can be accumulated and trends evaluated. (The variable set will be refined as we gain experience with modeling and data usage.) We seek increased participation in the survey—especially from the research universities, which are underrepresented in the current dataset.

The survey provides sufficient detail and a large enough sample size to permit a richer set of comparisons than can be covered in any publication. One could design a microcomputer database to aid survey respondents in making the best use of the data. Provided annually on a subscription basis, the database would allow institutional researchers to compare their own data for any survey variable against a profile for either predefined or custom-tailored institutional segments. A more advanced decision-support system would incorporate models to combine, transform, and project the data

Table 3.
Peterson's–AGB Strategic Indicators Survey Questionnaire
Major Headings and Selected Subheadings

Financial Profile

Revenue

Tuition and fee income

Government appropriations

Government grants and contracts

Private gifts, grants, and contracts

Endowment support for operations (payout or yield)

Sales and services of educational activities

Sales and services of auxiliary enterprises

Sales and services of hospitals

Other sources

Independent operations

Total revenue

Current expenditures by Function

Instruction (including departmental research)

Organized research

Public service

Academic support

Student services (excluding student aid awards)

Institutional support

Plant operation and maintenance

Expenditures on auxiliaries

Expenditures on hospitals

Expenditures on independent operations

Student financial aid

Total expenditures

Current expenditures by object

Wages and salaries [by type of employee]

Fringe benefits

Interest payments to outside entities

Balance Sheet

Assets

Current funds

Endowment book value

Plant and equipment

Other assets

Total assets

Liabilities and funds balances

Current liabilities

Short-term debt to outside entities

Long-term debt to outside entities

Funds balances

Total liabilities and funds balances

Physical Plant Detail

Financial

Beginning-of-year value

Depreciation for the year

Retirement of plant

Additions to plant (new construction)

End-of-year value

Plant Inventory and Condition

Gross square feet [by type of facility]

Estimated deferred maintenance backlog ($)

Libraries and Information Resources Detail

Library holdings

Book and monograph volumes

Journal subscriptions

Information resources

Microcomputers supplied for student use

Endowment Detail

Beginning-of-year market value [by fund type]

Return on investment [by type of return]

Other additions to endowment [by type]

Subtractions from endowment

Normal support for operations (from line 1.A.4)

Special uses (e.g., to cover deficits)

Total

End-of-year market value [by fund type]

Students

Fall enrollment [headcount & FTE, by level]

Fall FTE enrollment by EEOC category and level

Fall FTE enrollment by gender and level

Fall FTE enrollment by field of study and level

Degrees awarded by level

Admissions data for the full year

Number of applications

Number of offers of admission
Number of matriculants
Geographic dispersion of entering students by level
Number of states represented
Student headcount from home state
Students from outside the U.S. and Canada
Tuition and financial aid
Published charges
Financial aid headcounts by type of aid
Financial aid dollars by type of aid

Faculty and Staff
Faculty numbers [full and part time, by rank]
Regular faculty FTE
By field and rank
By EEOC category and rank
By gender and rank
Percent faculty over 60 years old
Faculty gains and losses for the year by rank
Headcount at the beginning of the year
In-hire
Voluntary termination
Termination by death or disability
Termination by the institution
Change category (e.g., non-tenured to tenured)
Headcount at the end of the year

Sponsored Research
Expenditures for organized research
U.S. Government [direct and indirect, by major agency]
State and local government agencies
Domestic corporations & corporate foundations
Other domestic private foundations
Foreign governments, corporations, foundations
Bequests and gifts from living individuals
Other outside sponsors
Institutional funds
Academic-year faculty salary offsets
Percent of regular faculty members who are principal investigators on sponsored projects
Research proposal and award statistics
Proposals sent to potential outside sponsors
Awards received from outside sponsors

Fund Raising [Other Than for Sponsored Projects]
Dollars raised during the year by source
Dollars raised during the year by use
Designated or restricted for current operations
Designated or restricted for student financial aid
Designated or restricted for endowment
Designated or restricted for plant
Percent of living alumni who are active donors (e.g., have given during the last five years)

elements for single schools or institutional segments. For example, a dynamic faculty cohort model could combine and transform data on hiring, tenure-granting, and retirement rates to project future tenure ratios, faculty age distributions, and longevity-based salary growth. Such models are well within the current state of the art.

CONCLUDING COMMENTS

This book's purpose is to raise issues of importance to higher education and to suggest ways for dealing with them. We are particularly interested in strategic issues that involve or should involve institutional leaders, and we will pursue these issues even when they challenge the conventional wisdom or threaten the industry status quo. Performance measurement and accountability represent quintessential examples of such issues.

I have argued that accountability is possible in higher education, that it is being mandated by our clients and sponsors, and that it is not incompatible with institutional, departmental, and faculty autonomy. I have raised questions about prestige maximization and the primacy of faculty research, and I hope that I have provided some useful ideas about how to evaluate quality and some insights about quantitative benchmark data. Although the ideas presented here represent only a beginning, I believe that the performance measures needed to track improvements in educational quality and institutional cost-effectiveness are well within our reach. Sustained creative effort and hard work by institutional leaders and their staffs will be required before colleges and universities can regain the public trust.

NOTES

1. *The Economist*, 1992, p. 18.

2. National Commission on Responsibilities for Financing Postsecondary Education, 1993, p. 56.

3. Bok, 1992, p. 16, emphasis added.

4. Massy and Zemsky, 1992; Policy Perspectives 1990; Zemsky and Massy 1990.

5. Boyer, 1987, p. 122.

6. Ibid., p. 121.

7. For further discussion, see Hopkins, 1990; Nerlove, 1972.

8. *The Economist*, 1992, p. 20.

9. Cf. Hammer, 1990.

10. Cell I: Boyer, 1991; Hoenack, 1974; Hoenack and Berg, 1980; Massy, 1989b; Policy Perspectives, 1989; Policy Perspectives, 1992.

Cell II: Massy, 1989a; Massy and Warner, 1991.

Cell III: Brown, 1988; Eble, 1972; Levin, 1989; Sherman, 1987; Stevens, 1988.

Cell IV: Baldridge, 1980; Griffin and Burks, 1976.

Cell V: Hyatt et al., 1984; Jedamus and Peterson, 1980; Massy, 1990a; Massy, 1990b; McGovern, 1988.

11. Massy, 1992.

12. Massy, 1989a.

13. Policy Perspectives, 1992.

14. "Teaching Quality," 1990, p. 5. The current controversy over educational quality measures in Britain postdates this inquiry.

15. Cross and Angelo, 1988.

16. AAU, 1988.

17. Massy, 1990c.

18. For an example in the overhead-rate domain, see Massy and Olson, 1991.

19. Massy and Zemsky, 1992.

20. Taylor et al., 1991.

21. See Little, 1970 for a classic discussion of the case for using explicit models even in qualitative situations.

22. Massy and Olson, 1991.

23. Hopkins and Massy, 1981, ch. 6, and Massy, 1990b.

24. Hopkins and Massy, 1981, ch. 8.

BIBLIOGRAPHY

"Teaching Quality: Report of the Committee of Enquiry Appointed by the Council." (1990). Polytechnics and Colleges Funding Council, Great Britain.

"Poisoned Ivy." (1992) *The Economist*, August 15, 18-20.

AAU (1988). "Indirect Costs Associated With Federal Support of Research on University Campuses: Some Suggestions for Change." AAU.

Baldridge, J. Victor (1980). "Managerial Innovation. Rules for Successful Implementation." *Journal of Higher Education* 15:117-134.

Bok, Derek (1992). "Reclaiming the Public Trust." *Change* (July-August):13-19.

Boyer, Ernest L. (1987). *The Undergraduate Experience in America*. New York: Harper & Row.

Boyer, E. L. (1991). *Scholarship Reconsidered: Priorities of the Professoriate*. Princeton, NJ: Carnegie Foundation for the Advancement of Teaching.

Brown, George (1988). *Effective Teaching in Higher Education*. London: Methuen.

Cross, K. Patricia and Thomas A. Angelo (1988). "The Classroom Research Project: Results of the First Ten Months. Progress report prepared for The Classroom Research Project." University of California, Berkeley.

Eble, Kenneth E. (1972). *Professors as Teachers*. San Francisco: Jossey-Bass.

Griffin, Gerald and David R. Burks (1976). *Appraising Administrative Operations: A Guide for Universities and Colleges*. Berkeley, CA: University of California.

Hammer, Michael (1990). "Reengineering Work: Don't Automate, Obliterate." *Harvard Business Review* (July-August):104-112.

Hoenack, S. A. (1974). "Incentives and Resources Allocation in Universities." *Journal of Higher Education* 45:21-37.

Hoenack, Stephen A. and David J. Berg (1980). "The Roles of Incentives in Academic Planning." *New Directions for Institutional Research* 28:73-95.

Hopkins, David S. P. (1990). "The Higher Education Production Function: Theoretical Foundations and Empirical Findings." In Stephen A. Hoenack and Eileen L. Collins (Eds.), *The Economics of American Universities*, pp. 11-32. Albany, NY: SUNY Press.

Hopkins, David S. P. and William F. Massy (1981). *Planning Models for Colleges and Universities*. Stanford, CA: Stanford University Press.

Hyatt, James A., Carol H. Shulman, and Aurora A. Santiago (1984). "Reallocation: Strategies for Effective Resource Management." National Association of Colleges and Business Officers.

Jedamus, Paul and Marvin W. Peterson (1980). *Improving Academic Management. A Handbook of Planning and Institutional Research*. San Francisco: Jossey-Bass.

Levin, Henry (1989). "Raising Productivity in Higher Education." Higher Education Research Program of the University of Pennsylvania and the Pew Memorial Trusts.

Little, John D. C. (1970). "Models and Managers: The Concept of a Decision Calculus." *Management Science* 16:466-85.

Massy, William F. (1989a). "Productivity Improvement Strategies for College and University Administrative and Support Services." Presented at the Forum for College Financing, held in Annapolis, MD (November).

Massy, William F. (1989b). "A Strategy for Productivity Improvement in College and University Academic Departments." Presented at the Forum for Postsecondary Governance, held in Santa Fe, NM (November).

Massy, William F. (1990a). "Budget Decentralization at Stanford University." *Planning For Higher Education* 18(2):39-55.

Massy, William F. (1990b). *Endowment: Perspectives, Policies, and Management*. Washington, DC: Association of Governing Boards of Universities and Colleges.

Massy, William F. (1990c). "Financing Research." In Richard E. Anderson and Joel W. Meyerson (Eds.), *Financing Higher Education in a Global Economy*. New York: ACE/Macmillan, pp. 41-56.

Massy, William F. (1992). "Beyond Responsibility Center Budgeting (working title)." Presented at the Conference on Resource Allocation and University Management in University of Southern California, Finance Center of the Consortium for Policy Research in Education, November 19-20.

Massy, William F. and Jeffery E. Olson (1991). "Overhead Diversity: How Accounting Treatments, Facilities Economics, and Faculty Salary Offsets Affect University Indirect Cost Rates." Stanford Institute for Higher Education Research, Stanford University, Discussion Paper.

Massy, William F. and Timothy R. Warner (1991). "Causes and Cures of Cost Escalation in College and University Administrative and Support Services." Presented at the National Symposium on Strategic Higher Education Finance and Management Issues in the 1990s in Washington DC, OERI and NACUBO, January 25, 1991.

Massy, William F. and Robert Zemsky (1992). "Faculty Discretionary Time: Departments and the Academic Ratchet." Stanford University, Stanford Institute for Higher Education Research, Academic Modeling Project Discussion Paper 4.

McGovern, James J. (1988). "Perspectives for Management Control and Program Budgeting." Medical College of Virginia, Virginia Commonwealth University, Report to the Deans.

National Commission on Responsibilities for Financing Postsecondary Education (1993), "Making College Affordable Again." Washington, DC: Final Report of the Commission (February).

Nerlove, Marc (1972). "On Tuition and the Costs of Higher Education: Prolegomena to a Conceptual Framework." *Journal of Political Economy*, Part II 3:S178-S218.

Policy Perspectives (1989). "The Business of the Business." 2(1). Philadelphia, PA: University of Pennsylvania, Pew Higher Education Research Program (May).

Policy Perspectives (1990). "The Lattice and the Ratchet." 2(4). Philadelphia, PA: University of Pennsylvania, Pew Higher Education Research Program (June).

Policy Perspectives (1992). "Testimony from the Belly of the Whale." 4(3). Philadelphia, PA: University of Pennsylvania, Pew Higher Education Research Program (September).

Sherman, Thomas, et. al. (1987). "The Quest for Excellence in University Teaching." *Journal of Higher Education* 58:66-84.

Stevens, Ellen (1988). "Tinkering with Teaching." *Review of Higher Education* 12:63-78.

Taylor, Barbara E., Joel W. Meyerson, Louis R. Morrell, and Dabney G. Park (1991). *Strategic Analysis*. Washington, DC: Association of Governing Boards of Universities and Colleges.

Zemsky, Robert and William F. Massy (1990). "Cost Containment." *Change* 22(6):16-22 (November-December).

Chapter 3

The Self-Transformation of Corporations: A Lesson from Industry?

Francis J. Gouillart

The business world is transforming itself. After spending most of the '80s playing financial restructuring games—one may remember this period as the buying and selling of America and Europe to itself—corporations are now turning to the more fundamental business of fixing what is broken with their competitiveness.

They do so under a curious proliferation of "new wave" names: reengineering, process redesign, renewal, transformation. All are aimed at describing a simple reality. Business involves "doing work" and "solving problems." And the way this work is performed and the way these problems are solved are often antiquated and ineffective. Repairing the way we "do work" and "solve problems" is therefore the first priority. And while the quality and continuous improvement movements of the early '80s were gradual and incremental, the transformational approaches are radical and discontinuous. Companies need to "reinvent themselves."

After the wave of pessimism of the late '80s, punctuated by the demise or occasionally the disappearance of large, historically successful companies—where are you, American Can, International Harvester and American Motors Corporation?—a few examples of successful revival of Western companies are beginning to emerge. The case for economic survival of the West seems to regain momentum. And many start copying these successful cases of transformation.

Ford is one such case. Under the leadership of Don Petersen, Ford's CEO from 1981 to 1990, Ford orchestrated a spectacular comeback. From a low profit company with a declining market share, Ford became in the late '80s the most profitable automotive company in the world. In 1989 Ford's profits even exceeded General Motors' in spite of GM's huge technology investments. Unheard of!

During that period Ford's marketshare regularly increased at a time when the collective market share of American manufacturers on their own continent continued to shrink against Japanese imports. In 1993 the Taurus, through its innovative design, achieved the status of best-selling car in the world, knocking the Honda Civic off its pedestal. Quality and reliability surveys also show that Ford is now close to Japanese standards.

General Electric is another example (see Tichy and Sherman). Jack Welch, its CEO, undertook a fundamental transformation of the company, starting in 1981. This proved particularly ambitious, given that General Electric, unlike Ford, was in good financial health at the time.

Jack Welch started with a merciless restructuring drive, earning him from *Business Week* the nickname "Neutron Jack." This first phase of Welch's tenure was capitalism at its rawest: layoffs, morale drops, drive to the bottom line.

By the mid-'80s, Welch gradually began to change his approach. After repairing the cost structure of multiple GE divisions, he started worrying about a new dimension of business life: change management. From pitiless enforcer he became an apostle of participation, making the Crotonville training center the cornerstone of his program to motivate and empower his employees. And from this apparent conversion of one of America's industrial captains came a new momentum for a mixture of "hard" techniques (i.e., ruthless pursuit of results) and "soft" approaches (i.e., relying on involving people in the drive to results).

Welch initiated a new organizational and problem-solving approach called "Work-Out." Simply stated, it involves sending scores of managers and employees to working sessions where the major problems of the corporation are discussed outside any organizational constraints. The term "work-out" has the double connotation of a sweaty exercise room and that of solving problems, as in "work out a solution." From hourly employees to top managers, all have the right to put problems on the table and to participate in their resolution. Managers have to act on the recommendations of the "Work-Out" sessions. These sessions rapidly proved effective at improving GE's overall ability to resolve complex issues.

And financial results shortly followed. General Electric today is extremely profitable and creates massive amounts of shareholder value.

The Saturn Division of General Motors constitutes a third example of successful transformation, once again in the automotive sector. Saturn is a ray of sunshine in an otherwise bleak environment for General Motors, managing to secure a healthy position at the lower end of the automotive product spectrum against entrenched Japanese competitors. After some early growing pains, the first models took off, leading America to regain confidence in its ability to manufacture.

Taking advantage of their ability to build everything from scratch, Skip LeFauve and his team reinvented all their work processes, including the development of a brand new distribution system. For the first time in the United States, Saturn cars are sold at a fixed rather than negotiated price. All studies point to the fact that car buyers, for the most part, do not enjoy the negotiation phase with the car dealer. But nobody had so far had the courage to change that phase. Saturn marked the end of car-buying trauma. Saturn also fundamentally rethought the manufacturing process, relying on team-based approaches, partnerships with suppliers, and continuous flow layouts.

Results proved spectacular. Saturn immediately found its market with former buyers of import vehicles. As was true for the Ford Taurus in the midsize range, the Japanese flow was stemmed once again. And early quality and reliability studies show Saturn to be a match for Japanese products from Toyota or Nissan.

Saturn also attributes its success largely to new working methods involving employee participation and the creation of compensation systems fostering problem-solving and team work. As a result, human resources departments across America are enjoying a second birth.

WHY TRANSFORMATION ATTEMPTS OFTEN FAIL: LESSONS FROM THE PAST

"What do CEOs think about?" one often wonders. Or more precisely, what are the issues CEOs deem most critical to the survival and flourishing of their company?

CEOs, it appears, worry about a broad set of issues (see *Reinventing the CEO*). They are authentic generalists of the business world. This is probably why they are paid huge sums of money.

When asked, CEOs often mention the stock price of their company and the overall profitability of the firm as key issues. The quality of their relationship with the investment community is often not far behind in their hit parade. Community relations are also high on the list. The most honest among them acknowledge that they care about their own compensation. The most altruistic give precedence to the competitive situation of their company. Many ask themselves what opportunities technology provides for them, particularly in the area of the management of information. Many are frustrated by their perception that their employees are unresponsive to customer needs and insufficiently attentive to quality issues.

Fundamentally, CEOs know that most of their problems can be traced back to people issues. But when one looks at a CEO's calendar, most of his or her time is not devoted to the development of people but to the management of crises: resignations, strikes, accidents, law suits, and many other forms of adversity.

Given this rainbow of issues, what do our CEOs do to address them?

CEOs create ad hoc programs. To tackle the stock price issue, they identify value-based planning methodologies and direct their chief financial officer to work with consultants on introducing such approaches into the firm. They also task the director of human resources to build new compensation systems. Anybody visiting manufacturing plants sees evidence of still other programs such as Total Quality Management, sponsored by vice-presidents for continuous improvement. Some plants are now "self-managed," with union and management making joint business decisions. The marketing director is often proud to sponsor his or her new "The Customer is King" program—or some equivalent program. And the MIS department has just started a complete revamp of its hardware and applications infrastructure.

All is well. We're being proactive. We are changing. We're preparing the next decade. And yet . . .

A few years later our same CEO is still at his desk, more frustrated than ever. "I'm moving and shaking everywhere I go," he laments. He lists with fervor all the initiatives taken in the last few years and confesses that the results of the corporation have not improved much. As he tries to understand what went wrong, he breaks into a long monologue.

"Maybe we're not working hard enough. It's probably this technological step we missed. Maybe this is attributable to the current recession, and it will go away. Probably our efforts will start paying off soon. Perhaps we should accelerate the pace of change. Now might be the right time to reorganize."

Our CEO is now caught in a trap. He has wasted a large part of his credibility by committing to a so far fruitless change program. But his only choice is to go on, trying to pick up the pace, in spite of the growing skepticism. To do so, he must further commit his personal credibility in the new wave of initiatives, exposing himself more and more to backlash. Like the squirrel in a rotating cage, all he can now do is run faster and faster.

In our experience the change model of our CEO suffers from three primary deficiencies:

- *Overwork for the firm's employees.* Many companies are dangerously approaching the breaking point with their employees. Many departments have seen their staff dramatically reduced in recent years. The early '90s have been characterized by a considerable increase in employee fatigue and depression, largely caused by the repeated waves of streamlining. All these new initiatives have piled up in the daily life of these already overworked employees, leading them to the brink of the abyss, and sometimes over it.

To understand this phenomenon, we highly recommend the practice of a small exercise called "Initiatives Review." Although simple, it often provokes insight. The exercise involves cataloging all the initiatives in progress in the firm at a particular point in time, i.e., all programs aimed at improving something in the way the organization operates. We then ask a few simple questions about each program. Who is the sponsor of the effort? What resources are committed to the effort? What are the expected results? How are results measured? When is the program slated to end?

From this low-technology tool one learns that managers and employees often spend from 30 to 40 percent of their time in initiatives of this type. More importantly, these initiatives, for the most part, have neither identified goals nor results-tracking systems associated with them, and as a result, they have an unlimited life expectancy and cost. Busy work, but also nefarious work through its consequences for the people inside the firm.

- *Lack of integration.* The map of initiatives in progress often resembles an inextricable jumbling of programs. Different programs compete for the same resources, generally the same "best people." The customer service and the quality programs both want the same product manager to "represent the customer" in their work teams. The same manufacturing engineer is wooed by both the reengineering and the new plant layout task force. Not to mention the fact that both people have a real job in civilian life, outside these programs.

Our product manager and manufacturing engineer would legitimately like to understand how these initiatives supplement and reinforce each other. But their queries only seem to meet the infinite silence of organizational disconnects. Each sponsor has his or her goals and only aims for one thing: become the sponsor of the highest impact initiative.

- *Lack of commitment of top management.* Program proliferation contributes to the development of a cynical organization. Today, quality. Tomorrow, service. Day after tomorrow, empowerment. Before you know it, employees start counting points in this war of the chiefs, with a "this too shall pass" attitude.

CEOs, like General Electric's Jack Welch making clear that "Work-Out" is "nonnegotiable," cannot afford to turn programs on and off—actually they turn them more often on than off. And yet, when they associate their names with a multitude of initiatives, they automatically dilute the credibility they lend to any one of them. If fifteen different programs can legitimately claim to be CEO-sponsored, the CEO will appear three or four times a year in support of each of them. The message becomes blurry: all is important and nothing is.

When a company exhibits this plethora of programmatic initiatives—and it may be the case for 80 percent of large U.S. corporations—the corporation starts vibrating throughout, agitated by a Brownian movement, trembling from all limbs . . . while staying put.

Consequently, our CEOs often have problems sleeping at night. To a large extent their sleeping ability largely depends on their ability to establish the right priorities. Unavoidably, executives learn that the toughest part of their job is to rally their employees around a limited set of goals and a set of convergent actions around these goals. The sketching of an integrated framework is the task we now turn to.

THE THREE OBJECTIVES OF BUSINESS TRANSFORMATION

Business transformation has three simultaneous objectives (see the diagram):

- The *reframing* of corporate issues
- The *restructuring* of the company
- The *revitalization* of the organization

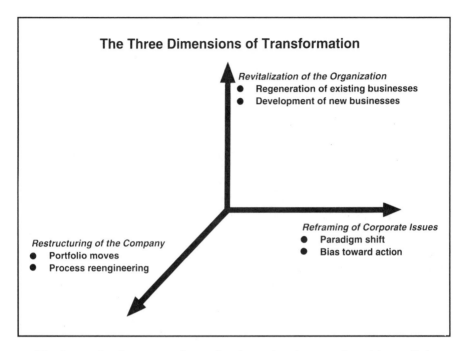

The key to business transformation is to simultaneously achieve all three objectives. Unlike the old Russian proverb stating that one cannot be simultaneously intelligent, communist, and sincere—one can only be two of the three at the same time—one must pursue all three objectives at once to achieve true transformation.

Simply *reframing* the issues of the corporation is intellectually satisfying but operationally frustrating. This is the shortcoming of traditional strategic planning: often appealing but impractical. Herein lies the strategic nightmare: 80 percent of all strategies fail. And the 20 percent that succeed, some caustic minds suggest, are developed by intuitive, uneducated self-starters.

Reframing is at the heart of many team-based initiatives. There are many corporate programs aimed at team building, focusing on exotic adventures such as white-water rafting or mountain climbing. Although they are occasionally helpful, these programs often fail to have the proper "content" focus and fail to address the question "What are we building the team around?" Consequently, the newly developed spirit often fails to find a practical application in the office or plant at the beginning of the following week.

Restructurings, in themselves, have a profoundly demotivating aspect. Without matching revitalization they wear down the company's body and mind, causing a morale drop and a loss of energy. High potential employees quickly understand that they are caught in a death spiral, and the company starts losing its best people. It is not easy, when one is a promising thirty-year-old engineer, to associate one's career with the fate of the American steel industry or commodity chemical industry.

Furthermore, restructurings without matching redesign of the work processes are effective only in the short term, ineffective in the longer term. Crude restructuring involves the blind application of personnel-reduction coefficients by departments without redesigning the work to be performed. In the short run, survivors often manage to handle the load with a reduced staff. In the middle and long term they often fail to do so. After a few months headcounts start going up again. "Streamlined" employees find their way back to the payroll, quickly renamed as "contractors" or "consultants."

Revitalization efforts, unless they are accompanied by a rationalizing of the associated cost structure, are pointless. There are few cases of companies that successfully revitalized without first restructuring their operations. Attempting to revitalize one's company without performing the necessary clean-up of the cost structure amounts to the proverbial building of a colossus with clay feet.

And revitalization without reframing can often be an illusion. There are numerous examples of corporations that bought high-technology, high-growth companies in the hope of reenergizing their core business—remember IBM's acquisition of Rolm, for example. To a large extent these attempts have failed—the acquirer has killed the acquired—largely because the necessary reframing did not occur or occurred in the wrong direction. The ill-fated incursions of Exxon into office equipment and of Mobil into mass distribution probably belong to this category.

REFRAMING CORPORATE ISSUES

The reframing of corporate issues comprises two parts:

- A *paradigm shift*. This is the conceptual part of transformation. Companies in trouble tend to dig their own graves, largely perpetuating the recipe that has so far led them to success. For Xerox, king of the copier business, or Philips, grand master of consumer goods electronics, it was hard to anticipate the impact that Canon, Fuji, or Sony would have on their market twenty years ago.

To succeed one must be able to articulate a fundamental purpose to the firm's actions, a statement of how the company is going to win, implying some stretched goals for the firm, and leveraging its core competencies (see Hamel and Prahalad). This is the "content" of strategy.

- A *bias toward action.* Having strategic objectives is one thing. Mobilizing the organization around these objectives is another. Behind the new strategic "content" one must also build a process that focuses all energies and results in concrete action. We now leave the ethereal world of conceptualization and enter the practical world of "things happening."

One of the toughest challenges in business transformation is to convince people that change is necessary. Even more difficult, one needs to convince people that not only must the company change, but that they themselves must change. From conceptual the message of change quickly starts hitting close to home. This change touches our daily life: a new job definition, perhaps a new location for our work, a less hierarchical mode of interaction with our subordinates, the budget possibly becoming less an instrument of power, maybe a growing demand for the development of interfunctional processes. All these can become dangerously concrete for our daily comfort. The fetid breath of change is upon our neck.

As was once again demonstrated recently in the Gulf War, mobilization becomes easier when the urgency is visible by all. President George Bush went from an approval rate of 90 percent in early 1991 to an electoral defeat in 1992 largely because the sense of emergency had vanished in the American mind. The challenge is to create a sense of urgency before one reaches an emergency, a difficult task.

Reframing involves the creative combination of paradigm shift and bias toward action. From this duality between content and process comes business transformation.

General Electric and Jack Welch changed both content and process in their transformation. Welch's strategic vision relies on four primary ideas.

First, each division must either be number one or number two in its market.

Second, each business must fit inside one of three "circles," symbolizing General Electric's three fundamental businesses: the "core business" of electrical equipment and derivatives, which includes businesses such as lighting, locomotives, or power plants; "technology businesses" such as medical equipment and aircraft engines; and "service businesses" such as financial services and information management. Other businesses, if they do not fit either of these three circles, are potential candidates for divestiture.

Third, General Electric operates on the principle of "integrated diversity." Each division is responsible for its own bottom line but at the same time benefits from its group affiliation. The "group effect" is obtained through personnel rotation across divisions, the dissemination of "best practices," or in some cases, an integrated offering across divisions. The integrated offering across divisions occurs when, for example, the financial services division helps the plastics division in securing an important automotive market where financing is a factor.

Fourth, each business must become global. This is for Welch a *sine qua non*. Any national competitor, he believes, is potentially exposed to outflanking by a global competitor picking up on a customer trend before you do or deriving worldwide economies of scale against you.

But Welch also believes in *mobilization* and *action*.

This first manifested itself through the creation of the Crotonville training center mentioned earlier. The "Work-Out" program is another example of the same reality, where the most sensitive issues are debated outside any organizational constraints. The program relies on teams as the primary vehicle for decision making and encourages confrontative problem solving as a way to reach closure on delicate matters. It also features global thinking in which international transfers are frequent, worldwide forums are encouraged, and a non-American experience is a precondition to any senior management advancement. This attitude also translates into a performance measurement system in which team spirit and bottom-line results are jointly rewarded.

In our mental model we tend to think of creativity as located in the "content" of strategy or the "what": the cleverness of Bill Gates creating Microsoft on the concept that software would one day capture the value of computer technology, not hardware. Or earlier the brilliant flash of insights of Henry Ford wanting to place every American behind the steering wheel of a Ford car.

But creativity manifests itself equally in the development of a transformation process, i.e., in the "how." All great top managers have created their own recipe for transformation, as have Jack Welch at General Electric, Don

Petersen at Ford, or Percy Barnevik at Asea Brown Boveri. Each successful story of large-scale change carries the fingerprints of its helmsman. It is as important in transforming a corporation to know which process to use as it is to identify the ultimate destination.

RESTRUCTURING THE COMPANY

Corporations must continually restructure. As stated in the latest aphorism of transformation, change is the only constant of our modern economic world. Restructuring, in particular, is a continuous, not a discrete, event.

Restructuring occurs simultaneously along two dimensions:

- Portfolio moves
- Process reengineering

Portfolio moves are necessary because companies constantly need to adjust their asset base. Managers must always be ready to sell certain parts of their business and acquire others. The value of each business changes continuously as a function of technological evolutions and other structural changes in the market. It is one of the manager's duties to seek to maximize the value of the corporate portfolio at all times.

Process reengineering is the operational equivalent of portfolio moves. Every business is a combination of functions, activities, and processes. For example, the order-to-delivery process in a manufacturing business involves entering the order, verifying credit, allocating the order to a set of machines, acquiring the raw material, physically making the parts, assembling the product, checking quality, transporting the product to the customer, invoicing the customer, and collecting the money.

Each process is characterized by a chronology of tasks, often supported by an infrastructure of other processes. In our order-to-delivery cycle, for example, we need a forecasting function that studies the historical pattern of orders coming in to ensure that we have the necessary raw material and personnel available when the actual order arrives. We also need a scheduling process that analyzes how to allocate the orders received to the various machines so as to minimize both cost and lead time to delivery.

Each process unfolds in the context of a system made up of:

- An *organization* in which roles and responsibilities have been distributed among departments and people

- An *infrastructure*. For example, how many machines and plants are available to produce against a particular order?
- A set of *metrics*. How is the performance measured in relation to this process? What are we trying to accomplish, and how do we measure the output of our process?
- A *performance measurement system*. What are we rewarding or punishing in the execution of this process?
- A set of *technology requirements*. What technologies are available to support this process, either in the manufacturing technology or information technology area?
- A set of *skills*. What skills are available to complete the process?

Each process and its associated system needs to continually adjust to stimuli in the environment. This, in turn, requires all dimensions associated with the work also to change with the process. But because these processes change all the time, there is often little time for orderly and simultaneous modification of all elements of the system. The organization starts getting in the way of the process, the computer systems cannot adapt fast enough, and behaviors are rewarded that work at cross-purpose from the new process. As a result, a multitude of Band-aids are hastily placed on the original process, transforming what was once a lean and nimble process into an obese and inflexible set of misaligned elements.

Like a body that rapidly accumulates fat, a corporation must constantly exercise. It must review its working processes, as well as the organizational, informational, and technological environments in which it exists. And with great humility the company must periodically check whether its processes remain consistent with "best practices" inside and outside its industry.

At General Electric Jack Welch is a master at both portfolio moves and process reengineering.

Between 1981 and 1991 Welch sold a large number of businesses, moving out of consumer electronics (particularly televisions), defense, air conditioning, mining, and many other businesses. Conversely, he acquired multiple other businesses in medical equipment, financial services, and others.

These divestitures and investments have largely followed the strategic guidelines set by Welch. Divested entities have involved businesses that neither fit into the three-circle approach previously described nor had much hope of ever becoming number one or number two in their markets.

The early restructuring at GE was done without much attention to process reengineering. In the last six years, however, process reengineering has become second nature at GE. GE employees have learned to characterize their "as is" processes and know how to redefine "to be" processes to reduce cost, increase effectiveness, and produce better results for their customers. Between 1981 and 1991 Welch is estimated to have reduced the total number of jobs at GE by 170,000 people (not counting another 135,000 who went with the divested businesses).

REVITALIZING THE ORGANIZATION

To speak as a logician, restructuring is a necessary but not sufficient condition for companies to succeed. In themselves restructurings do not lead to financial results. It is hard to save oneself into prosperity. And restructurings, in themselves, do not amount to a strategy—although it sometimes feels that way when listening to some CEOs. At some point, the company must create some *growth* and start working on the *revenue* part of the equation.

As was true for restructuring, revitalization involves two components:

- Regeneration of existing businesses
- Development of new businesses

The *regeneration of existing businesses* postulates that any business offers pockets of operational improvements on the revenue side.

The pricing process is often a source of dramatic improvements once companies start realizing how much they leave on the table through successive discounts. Many companies believe that prices are the outcome of an objective bargaining process between their customers and themselves. But experience shows that prices are often random, largely driven by the quality of the sales force and negotiating skills on both sides, rather than by the volume actually purchased or the overall strategic importance of the customer to the firm.

In the production area it is often possible to increase the effective capacity of a machine or set of machines, for example, by reducing the changeover or setup time between batches or orders. The same result can often be obtained by reallocating the products to the various machines, focusing each machine on a narrower set of products. This results in a volume increase without matching investment and can constitute a significant source of additional revenues if the added output can find a market.

The allocation of salespeople's time is also a source of potentially significant revenue increase. Many sales forces spend a considerable amount of time on internal support tasks, checking orders, making appointments, verifying either commissions or the status of orders. Through a judicious reallocation of time between the client-facing and the internal component, one can often increase revenues significantly.

The *development of new businesses* is ultimately the best form of revitalization, however.

The idea is a simple one. Most of the growth in corporate entities does not occur within existing businesses but at the intersection between businesses (see Hamel and Prahalad). More specifically, it happens when two or more core competencies, typically located across businesses, meet to give birth to a brand-new business.

NEC, for example, through its unique marriage of computer and communication technology, was able to challenge both IBM and AT&T despite being originally a very small competitor against those two. Canon, through its optical and small engine know-how coming from the photographic business, was able to break into the copying business when Xerox's position looked so intimidating that Canon, according to traditional strategic precepts, should never have succeeded.

GE's Jack Welch is an ardent supporter of tackling cost and revenue issues simultaneously. Until now, however, he has enjoyed greater success in the regeneration of existing businesses than in the outright creation of new businesses. And therein may lie his challenge for the next few years.

GE's lighting division is a success story for the revitalization of an existing business. Since Edison invented the light bulb, the lighting division had maintained an acceptable level of profitability and a dominant, albeit slowly declining, marketshare in the United States.

In a few years time its president, John Opie, working closely with Welch, undertook a systematic restructuring program involving the divestment of its machine engineering department, which had become uncompetitive; a dramatic increase in outside sourcing of components, as opposed to internal manufacturing; and the reduction of about 6,000 jobs.

Revitalization also largely occurred through globalization. While the lighting business was considered regional by most competitors, GE proceeded to challenge Philips right in its home turf in Europe. It first purchased Tungsram in Hungary, then the light bulb division of Thorn EMI in the UK. Although it is still too early to judge the results of this globalization drive, the lighting division at GE is clearly enjoying a second birth.

GE's performance in the area of interdivisional growth is a less glamorous one, although Welch is now also promoting its merits. Over the years General Electric has dismantled what could have been a powerful consumer electronics set of businesses. Through its electronic components business, its television business, its appliance business, and its information management know-how, GE could have become an American Sony or Matsushita. Instead, it treated every business as a standalone, failing to recognize the potential power of their interaction.

A CHALLENGE FOR WESTERN CORPORATIONS

Recent surveys show that American and European CEOs consider restructuring issues, most notably quality and service, to be their number one priority (see *Reinventing the CEO*). Japanese managers, by contrast, consider the invention of new businesses to be their first agenda item. In even more worrisome fashion for European and American CEOs, preoccupations of quality and service were on the agenda of Japanese CEOs five or ten years ago. Today, Japanese CEOs consider those problems to be largely solved. Are Western CEOs working hard at developing the great firms of yesterday?

There is little doubt that the revitalization and reframing dimension of transformation will gradually take precedence over the restructuring dimension in the latter part of the century. Growth will constitute the new frontier, not how well you know how to restructure. Restructuring will probably become a "commodity" skill, mastered by all. Companies that know how to do both restructuring and revitalization will thrive. Companies that only know how to restructure will demonstrate how to manage one's downfall.

The future belongs to those corporations that will reinvent themselves continuously.

REFERENCES

Reinventing the CEO, 21st Century Report, A Global Study Conducted Jointly by Korn/Ferry International and Columbia University Graduate School of Business, Vol. 1, No. 1, 1989.

Hamel, G., and C. K. Prahalad, "Strategic Intent," *Harvard Business Review*, May-June 1989.

Ibid., "The Core Competence of the Corporation," *Harvard Business Review*, May-June 1990.

Tichy, N. M., and S. Sherman, *Control Your Destiny or Someone Else Will: How Jack Welch is Making General Electric the World's Most Competitive Corporation*, Doubleday/Currency, 1993.

Chapter 4

New Dangers in Old Traditions: The Reporting of Economic Performance in Colleges and Universities[1]

Gordon C. Winston

How do colleges and universities describe their economic performance—their economic well-being—to themselves, their board and faculty members, the public? Not the way you'd expect, with direct answers to the questions that tell us whether the college had a good year or a bad year. Instead, we use "fund accounting." This article does two things. One is to express a growing suspicion that while fund accounting has long been an irritant to those dealing with college finances, it's in the process of becoming downright dangerous as the circumstances of colleges and universities change. The other is to describe a different way of picturing our economic performance—through "global accounts."

FUND ACCOUNTING

The convention in college accounting—indeed, the requirement—is to use Fund Accounts. The activities of the college are divided up into little individual *firms* each of which has its own accounts—balance sheet and income statement (known as "Fund Balances" and "Statement of Changes in Fund Balances"). These little firms are differentiated by *purpose*—one for endowment affairs, one for plant and equipment, one for current spending, and so on. They're like the envelopes my mother used to separate the food money from the clothing and entertainment money and the savings. The justification for keeping these funds separate in a college is *stewardship*. Recognizing that much of the money a college gets comes from

71

donors or legislators who have definite purposes in mind, fund accounting provides a way of monitoring the college's performance against those donors' desires. So fund accounting has a useful role to play.

But there are serious problems with using fund accounting to describe the economic performance of a college. They are two, and they're closely related.

Most important, *fund accounts are simply very hard to understand.* Seven or more little fictitious firms are described, each with its separate Fund Balances and Statement of Changes of Fund Balances and, central to the confusion, with a set of flows and obligations between and among them in the form of mandatory and nonmandatory and temporary transfers and loans and borrowing that leave the IOUs issued by one part of the college in the asset portfolio of another part. Nowhere is this all put together to tell what the college, *as a whole*, has been up to.

The result is that without, literally, years of effort and experience, ordinary mortals like board and faculty members and, indeed, administrators can't make a lot of sense of fund accounts—they can't get from them a picture of what's going on in the college as a whole.

Which leads to the second problem. The result of this incomprehensibility of our accounts is the natural one—that we've cut the issue down to size by focusing on only *part* of the college's economic activity—the operating budget and endowment—*as if it were the whole thing*. We can't get our minds around that complicated description of the whole economic situation, so we do the next best thing by understanding a part of it. But it's only part. And it's a manipulable part. At Williams, to take the example I know best, the operating budget over the years has included only about two-thirds of the college's total economic activity. The rest is, one way or another, "off budget," and what is included in the budget can, within wide limits, be changed at will. As for the endowment, it includes about half the assets of a rich college—and none of its liabilities.

At some level, everybody knows this. Despite the fact that newspapers report the budget deficits and surpluses of the major universities as if they were news, everybody knows that they're not the whole story—that there are mysterious other resources being got and spent by the college with names like "unavailed endowment earnings" and "gifts to plant" and "bond sale proceeds." But it's never clear where or how much.

Which brings me to my worry. These economic mysteries may be tolerable in ebullient times that bring more resources and expanded staff and more programs and higher salaries in colleges and universities. But when times turn stringent, as they certainly have in the past few years, such obscurity is too easily seen as obfuscation—evidence of hanky panky by the administration or board that's intended to wring unnecessary concessions from one group on campus or another, or from taxpayers. We've got a whole generation of faculty (and young administrators) who have never seen anything but the lush 1980s and a larger number who have persuaded themselves that the expansions of the eighties were normal. And public institutions have to contend with legislators who are trying to survive in a period of generalized tax revolt: "Read My Lips." The fundamental challenge to college administrations over the next few years, arguably, will be to induce a highly resistant community to understand that there's an economic reality within which they'll have to live, one that may include "downsizing" and "restructuring" and the biting of all sorts of personally painful bullets. This is *not* an atmosphere in which obscurity about total institutional resources will be helpful.

It's possible that in a time of more rigid institutional hierarchies, suspicion of the mystery-resources that are hidden by fund accounting might have been limited to grumbles in the Faculty Club or legislative cloak room. But we are increasingly people whose first automobiles carried "Challenge Authority" bumper stickers, and we're less likely to be simply glum and docile in the face of "restructuring." Wide participation in these decisions, invited or not, seems inevitable. And it's not reasonable to expect people to become competent in deciphering the economics of fund accounting. So the only recourse of administrations, really, has been to say "trust us" when every community instinct is not to.

So fund accounting has, in this worried view, moved by force of the changing circumstances of higher education from being an issue of bookkeeping to impinging importantly on university morale and governance.

Before looking at the alternative to fund accounting, let me be clear that the quarrel here is not with fund accounting per se. It is with the use of fund accounting as the *primary* way of describing the economic performance and circumstances of an institution. Fund accounting is undeniably useful: responsible stewardship is important in nonprofit institutions that depend on the charity of donors and taxpayers—we have an obligation to monitor the use of those resources with care. But it's the tail wagging the dog if we use those stewardship accounts as the primary description of how the college is doing.

GLOBAL ACCOUNTS

An alternative way of describing the economic performance of a college grew, literally, out of the frustrations of one of those typical faculty-administration-student committees—The Committee on Priorities and Resources at Williams—that was supposed to advise the college on its economic policies. It quickly became clear that Ph.D economists with training in accounting simply couldn't make ready economic sense of the numbers. The conviction grew increasingly strong that we *should* be able to see—easily—the answers to simple questions like how much the college took in in a given year and what it did with it. What came of the effort to answer those questions was a reorganization of our economic information that proved useful at Williams and can help, too, at larger and different places. There's every indication that it will travel well.

There were two overriding objectives in this reorganization of the college's economic information, two guiding obsessions. That it be *clear* and that it be *complete*. So the new system really is the direct result of fund accounting's problems; if fund accounting information is intractable and balkanized, we wanted to devise a way of telling the story that was accessible and encompassing, that described the whole of the college and did it simply, a "global" description of the institution's economic fortunes. The two things fund accounts aren't. So, "*Global* Accounts."

We wanted to wind up with a set of accounts that answered the question: "Did the year's activities make the college better off or worse off economically?" When the global accounts are used as the basis of an economic plan, that question becomes "Will the behavior and policies we're considering now make the college better off or worse off in the future?" Harvard's recently remodeled financial report poses a similarly basic question: "Did Harvard have a good year or a bad year?"[2]

I should note my considerable delight in Harvard's radical change in its economic reporting because it is so clearly in the same spirit as these global accounts and with the same purposes. Harvard didn't go as far—in the direction of clarity and completeness—as do global accounts, but they had a good deal more at stake in changing the system. So these global accounts can be seen as going all the way, as the end-point in the process toward which Harvard is moving. Clearly Harvard's decision will make it easier for the rest of us to make these kinds of changes. As of their March 1992 financial report, these ideas suddenly became a good deal less academic and a lot more practical.

Now let me try to give you a quick picture of the global accounts, to describe their major features—the implications of this assiduously simple-minded approach—and the kinds of policy questions they lead to, both as global *accounting* of past performance and as a global *economic plan* that describes the future impact of current decisions. (There is a detailed description of them in the summer issue of *Planning*.[3])

Three quite simple Econ 101 questions structure these accounts:

1. How much did the college take in during the year—from all sources?
2. What did it do with that money?
3. What effect did all that have on its real wealth[4]—in total?

That's it. For the whole of the college, taken all together, year by year.

The emphasis on creating a *complete accounting* takes us farther than might be expected, however. Income comes into a college by many routes, reported in many funds, and the route often depends on local accounting traditions. And current spending is usually spread throughout the funds: much in the current fund, but some in the plant fund and often more in the endowment fund. Ferreting these out is neither easy nor impossible.

But the biggest impact on a system of accounts of the determination to be complete is in the accounting of wealth and saving (as changes in wealth). It is there that conventional accounting leaves out the most with its focus on *financial* wealth and relative disregard of *physical capital* wealth.

Global accounts address the neglect of physical wealth by (a) reporting the value of plant, equipment, and land in its *current*, replacement value rather than its historical book value, (b) reporting its *actual* depreciation during the year, and (c) recognizing that that *depreciation is a current cost of production*. While the proper accounting of capital costs in nonprofit institutions is a subject in itself,[5] knowledge of these three facts is essential before we can answer the "Are we better off or worse off?" question or know how much our education costs. These are the changes Harvard has made in its economic reporting (even though doing it added $77 million to reported operating costs and led to a $42 million reported deficit). The fact Harvard has recognized—the fact that's embedded in the global accounts—is that using up one's physical capital is an unavoidable current cost of production, and failure to recognize that fact, in full, will lead inevitably to an understatement of the current costs of education and potentially, down the road, to an accumulation of deferred maintenance.[6]

In keeping with the Econ 101 simplicity of the global accounts, *saving* is, as in Econ 101, just the difference between total income and total current spending for the year. Saving can take either a financial form—adding to money in the bank or financial investments—or a physical form—adding new buildings or property or lab equipment. Both of these kinds of assets are measured in global accounts by the same yardstick: current market value for financial assets and current replacement values for physical assets. So they can be added together to get (adjusted for liabilities and deferred maintenance) a picture of the institution's total net worth: the whole of its wealth in both financial and physical forms.

At Williams in 1991, to give some sense of magnitudes in accounting for all of a college's wealth, to $309 million of financial wealth was added $335 million of physical capital wealth, making the college's total wealth some $644 million. Judging from Harvard's reported figures, its $5.9 billion of financial wealth was only part of a total wealth of $8.2 billion.[7] Impressionistic figures from Yale[8] also suggest that physical capital wealth just about doubles—even for these kinds of wealthy private institutions—reported financial wealth. And of course, the poorer the school, the larger the share of its wealth will be in the form of physical capital.

So in global accounts, a year's *saving* is the thing to watch. More income or less current spending increases the year's saving. Saving increases the college's wealth. Dis-saving decreases it. And since these are complete, exhaustive, global measures, anything that increases income increases wealth; anything that increases current spending reduces wealth. Anything that simply changes the *form* of wealth leaves its total level unchanged.

So, for example, if a college uses $10 million of quasi-endowment to build a $10 million dormitory, its total wealth is unchanged; the form of its wealth is changed (as are future income and costs), but not the total amount. If the college borrows to build that dorm, both physical and financial wealth are changed but, again, not the total. If too little is spent on maintenance of plant and equipment, total wealth falls and the value of physical wealth goes down. If current spending goes up, wealth goes down; if income goes up, wealth goes up. These are simple but immensely important facts about economic performance.

Most basically, saving allocates resources to future generations, spending allocates them to the present generation.

Global accounts describe the impact of the college's actions on its total real wealth. The proverbial bottom line of global accounts is just that: the effect of a year's activities on the college's total real wealth.

Where does that leave the usual bottom line of conventional accounting—*operating budget* deficits and surpluses? There *isn't* an operating budget in the global accounts. Operating *expenditures*—as a centrally important part of costs—*are* reported, but the fiction of an operating *budget* per se is abandoned as being more misleading than helpful. Operating expenses are reported prominently and should be closely monitored to see if they exceed or fall short of projected spending. But the fiction of a budget deficit or surplus, resulting from the arbitrary assignment of some part of income to an operating budget under the name of "operating revenues," can best be done away with as arbitrary, manipulable, and meaningless.

So much for global accounts as an economic description of a year's activities, as accounting of the *past*.

As the basis for an *economic plan*, or projection of the future, global accounts are particularly useful. A global economic plan is a quite simple extension, taking advantage of the two fundamental tautologies of accounting: (1) that a year's saving equals income minus current spending, always, and (2) that net worth at the beginning of the year plus saving has to equal net worth at the end of the year. These two facts fit neatly into a spreadsheet to drive a nice, simple economic planning model. It's not a financial equilibrium model, though it can show that; it's more than financial and less than equilibrium. It's certainly not an optimizing model. It's really, simply, a *consistency* model—it makes the constraints and the implications of plans, policies, and behavior dynamic in order to answer the general question "If you do that now, what will the future look like?"

The global economic plan we've used at Williams is grounded in actual performance in the most recent years, it makes explicit intended behavior and anticipated circumstances, and it describes their implications for future saving and wealth. We used two years' historical base, the current year's budgeted performance, and a description of the future plans, behavior, and circumstances we thought reasonable. From that we generated their implications for saving and wealth over the next three years (we also looked ten years out to see whether anything subtle was going on that didn't show up immediately). So the planning exercise began with recent history that set its initial levels of income and spending and described recent trends in growth, and it projected the implications of the plans, policies, and circumstances we were thinking of.

Finally, let me suggest some of the facts about the college's economic performance on which global accounts will focus attention. At the most basic level, the information of these accounts is agnostic—it can inform a whole lot of quite different policies—but some things are easier to see than others. These are questions—six of them—that have helped focus policy discussions at Williams:

1. What was the *effect of the year's activities* (and circumstances) on the college's total wealth: how much did it save or lose?

2. How much did *inflation* erode the purchasing power of the college's wealth: how much did it have to save just to offset the effects of inflation? Did it do it?

3. How much of their saving—or dis-saving—was in *financial* assets and how much in *physical* assets? (Financial assets are seen to earn money; physical assets are seen to cost money.[9])

4. Some of the *gifts* to the college were intended by their donors to increase the value of its wealth: gifts to endowment and plant. Taking those donor intentions seriously means subtracting that amount from total saving to answer: How *would* the college have done without those gifts?

5. How much did the wearing out of physical capital—*depreciation*—contribute to the current costs of education?

6. How much of that depreciation was *not* met by spending on renovations and adaptation during the year; in other words, how much additional *deferred maintenance* did the college incur during the year?

These questions suggest the kinds of facts about economic performance that are revealed by global accounts. In a global economic plan these same questions are asked about some future date in consequence of policies under current consideration: "If we maintain faculty salary increases at levels of the past three years without reductions in their FTEs, what will be the answers, three years from now, to questions 1-6?" or "If we expand dormitory space by $10 million . . ." Etc.

CONCLUSION

Four brief comments may be useful in conclusion.

First, the global accounts are a direct reaction to the shortcomings and frustrations of fund accounting. Because fund accounts are opaque and balkanized, global accounts were designed to be clear and complete. Global accounting is intended to go all the way toward clarity and completeness[10] as a logically consistent aggregate description of the college's economy. They're an idealized aggregate account, but one that's proved surprisingly workable—a rare, practical ideal, it seems.

But second, a college doesn't have to go all the way in order to benefit from the global accounts. It is useful to go only part way, to sneak up on completeness while gaining in clarity. So a *Global Financial Account* reorganizes reporting of the financial side while sticking to a conventional treatment of physical capital wealth. That's what Williams has done. Alternatively, a college can do a global accounting of physical capital wealth while treating the financial variables pretty conventionally. That's what Harvard has done. A lot is gained by the full treatment, but this is a case where something is better than nothing—more clarity and more completeness, even if still short of ideal, are worth it.

Third. For the time being, at least, global accounting has to be an overlay, reported on top of conventional, audited, fund accounts.[11] It is unrealistic to expect accounting and auditing conventions to change as quickly as we—for reasons of governance—need our reported information to change. So global accounts can't replace fund accounts. A more enduring reason, perhaps, is the fact that by staying simple, global accounts have to leave out a whole lot. We tried hard at Williams to keep the whole of the global accounts to a single page, printed landscape at that. So lots of more disaggregated information is needed for more specific purposes: like stewardship and benefit management and department budgets and monitoring personnel costs and running academic programs and . . . Even here, though, when such subaccounts are fitted into the aggregate framework, global accounts will show the implications of changes within them. Changes throughout the college will be connected.

Finally, a very practical fact. A global economic plan, in a Lotus or Excel spreadsheet, fits on a laptop computer that can easily go into meetings on downsizing and restructuring, or just into discussions of next year's operating expenditures. The economic constraints within which those discussions have to operate are made explicit. They're clear and understandable—even intuitive—without a whole lot of personal investment. So even "nonquantitative" members of a faculty or a board can see clearly what's at stake. Through them there is instant access to the implications of alternative policies and programs, or different circumstances.

Clearly there are some disadvantages to all this clarity. A familiar and comforting administrative discretion and control over economic information is obviously lost with the openness—the transparency—of global accounts. Many will see Pandora's Box. But aside from arguments in favor of an open management style per se, if my worst suspicions are right, that loss of control will prove a small price to pay for a more realistically and completely informed—and hence more effective, less suspicious, and less confrontational—college as we face the hard job of scaling expectations back.

NOTES

1. The research for this chapter was supported by the Andrew W. Mellon Foundation through its assistance to the Williams Project on the Economics of Higher Education. To appear in *Change*, January/February, 1993.

2. Harvard University, *Financial Report to the Board of Overseers of Harvard College For the Fiscal Year 1990-91*. Cambridge: The Harvard University Press; 1992. p. 4.

3. Gordon C. Winston, "The Necessary Revolution in Financial Accounting," *Planning for Higher Education*, Summer 1992, pp. 1-16.

4. "Wealth" is not the happiest word here. It accurately describes the institution's stock of resources, but it connotes ease and luxury. Harvard uses "equity" and, of course, "net worth" is the for-profits phrase that describes it. In this paper I'll stick to "wealth" and "net worth," but with acknowledged discomfort and a hope for advice on a better alternative.

5. Gordon Winston, "The Capital Cost Conundrum: Why Are Capital Costs Ignored?" *NACUBO Business Officer*, April, 1993.

6. The recently mandated depreciation accounting of FASB 93 is, arguably, a step in the wrong direction; it is certainly a step in the other direction from the global accounts. A college could scrupulously follow the FASB rules for a decade—setting aside an appropriate amount for depreciation each year—and wind up with far more deferred maintenance than funds to do something about it. The problem is their (understandable) reliance on book values for the capital stock. These historical costs typically so understate the current replacement values of plant and equipment that the depreciation calculated on them understates real depreciation seriously. Nor does FASB require that depreciation be shown as an operating cost—it need only be a downward adjustment to an already understated value of the capital stock.

7. Note that this is capital measured (a) at replacement cost and (b) reduced by accumulated deferred maintenance, as in the Williams numbers. Too, all financial assets are included, not just endowment.

8. Henry Hansmann, "Why Do Universities Have Endowments?" *Journal of Legal Studies*, vol. XIX, January, 1990, pp. 3-42.

9. This is part of current conventions, but see my Discussion Paper 14 cited in Note 5.

10. Once again, *almost* all the way. Important capital costs are, in this version of the global accounts, still left out (Gordon Winston, "The Capital Cost Conundrum: Why Are Capital Costs Ignored?" *NACUBO Business Officer*, April, 1993).

11. So Harvard has had to adjust the reported value of its capital stock back, in its financial accounts, to historical values.

Chapter 5

Benchmarking—How Good Is Good?

Sean C. Rush

You are the president of one of the country's leading overnight delivery services. Each business day 2.5 million packages containing contracts, proposals, and other important documents are entrusted to your company for "next day delivery" to virtually all cities and towns within the continental United States. Your commitment to your customers is simple: guaranteed overnight delivery at a reasonable price. During the past five years your delivery volume has increased by 25 percent, growing from 2 million packages to the current 2.5 million. In each of those five years, 99 percent of all packages arrive at the right destination at the right time. Your company is profitable. And from all appearances it is successful . . . or is it?

In assessing your company's market position, you discover that your primary competitor's package delivery volume has grown by 30 percent to 1.8 million packages per day during the last two years and that their pricing is about 10 percent below your company's average price. Further analysis reveals that your competitor delivers 99.9 percent of all packages to the right place at the right time. In short, they are doing a better job at a lower price . . . and they are profitable. Your own customer surveys indicate that price is not the primary determinant in selecting a delivery service. Service quality and reliability are the key factors. With a 99 percent success rate you believe your company has done an excellent job. Is a 0.9 percent differential in delivery quality enough to make a difference?

In fact, it could make a huge difference.

With a 99 percent success rate for 2.5 million packages per day, your company has 2.475 million satisfied customers a day. However, it also has 25,000 *dissatisfied* customers. If the definition of "customer" is expanded to include both the sender and the receiver of the package, the numbers swell to 50,000 unhappy customers per day; 250,000 per week, and 12.5

million per year (assuming no overlaps). Your competitor, on the other hand, is "dissatisfying" only 3,600 customers per day, 18,000 per week, and 900,000 per year. If service reliability and quality are the key determinants in selecting a delivery company, there is a considerable gap between the performance of the two companies.

	Volume/ Day	Success Rate	Unhappy Customers		
			Day	Week	Year
Your company	2.5 MM	99.0%	50,000	250,000	12,500,000
Your competitor	1.8 MM	99.9%	3,600	18,000	900,000
Gap	+ .7 MM	<.9%>	<46,400>	<232,000>	<11,600,000>

Delivery Company "Gap" Analysis

On top of discovering that you "dissatisfy" nearly 14 times more customers than your competitor each day, you have also learned that your company's delivery cost per package is 10 percent higher than your competitor's. In essence, it is costing you 10 percent more per package to "dissatisfy" 14 times as many people. How does your competitor do it? And, unfortunately, how do you do it?

Although the preceding scenario is a fictitious but not improbable situation, it provides an excellent demonstration of how the concept of *benchmarking* can reshape one's thinking about the performance and operations of an organization. Benchmarking is an ongoing, systematic process for measuring and comparing the work processes of one organization to another by bringing an external focus on internal activities, functions, or operations. The purpose of benchmarking is to provide managers with an external point of reference or standard for evaluating the quality and cost of their organization's internal activities, practices, and processes. In all cases benchmarking strives to provide an organization with a demonstrable cost or quality advantage by replacing management intuition or "gut feel" with facts and analysis that foster the best operational practices.

Simply described, benchmarking attempts to answer the following questions:

- How well are we doing compared to others?
- How good do we want to be?
- Who's doing the best?
- How do they do it?

- How can we adapt what they do to our institution?
- How can we be better than the best?

In the case of our delivery company, intuition and "gut feel" were leading one company into difficulty. Although management was proud of its 99% success rate on deliveries, it had failed to ask one fundamental question about its delivery performance: *Compared to what?* Lacking an external yardstick to truly measure the quality of delivery service, a company could easily be lulled into a false sense of success while other companies were gobbling up its disaffected customers. Compounding the service quality problems at the delivery company was the finding that the competing company had achieved its higher quality at a 10 percent lower cost. In short, they had a better mousetrap.

Benchmarking in one form or another has been around for several millennia, if not more. In his book *Benchmarking* Robert Camp cites one of the many rules established by the Chinese general Sun-Tzu in 500 B.C.: "If you know your enemy and know yourself, you need not fear the result of a hundred battles." Resisting the obvious temptation to equate modern day business commerce with military strategy, the 2,500-year-old thought of General Sun-Tzu nonetheless holds true. Call it competitive analysis, strategic position assessment, or corporate "espionage," American business has historically spent a fair amount of time trying to discern "what the other folks are up to." Many in the corporate world argue with Socrates that knowing oneself is only half of the equation. Knowing the competition is the other half.

During the past fifteen years, however, the old idea of knowing the competition (the "enemy" to Sun-Tzu) has taken on a distinctly sharper focus. Increasingly, corporations and other organizations are using benchmarking as a pivotal tool in strategic, operational, and organizational change. It is being used to dramatically transform how organizations view themselves and conduct their business. The use of benchmarking as such a tool emerged in the late 1970s at Xerox Corporation. In *Benchmarking: A Tool for Continuous Improvement* K.H.J. Liebfried and C.J. McNair describe the benchmarking experience of Xerox:

> During the 1980s, Xerox Reprographics Manufacturing Group had a continuous improvement program that was achieving an 8 percent productivity increase over a period of years. One Sunday afternoon, however, Charles Christ, president of the Group, saw an ad in the *New York Times* for copiers that were essentially the same, in terms of function

and performance, as the ones he was building in Webster, New York. These copiers were selling at retail for less than he could manufacture them! At about the same time there was an article in *Fortune* that quoted the president of Canon claiming he was going to wage total war on Xerox and was going to win.

"This was a turning point. It made me realize we had greater problems than we had anticipated," Christ recounted. "We had been very successful [in the late 1960s Xerox developed a flagship product—the 914 copier—and had 80 percent of the marketshare by the mid-1970s]; we had lost that and now we were fighting, in a sense, for the market that we had established." Xerox stock was at an all-time low and marketshare had dropped to the low 30s.

In response, Christ sent a team of manufacturing people to Japan to study, in great detail, the process, the product, and the material. His parting words to the team were, "I need a benchmark, something that I can measure myself against to understand where we have to go from here." This competitive benchmarking resulted in specific performance targets rather than someone's guess or intuitive feel of what needs to be done—which is the real power of the process. Quality went from 91 defects per 100 machines to 14. Line fallout (defined as bad parts on the line) went from 30,000 per million parts to 1,300 per million. There was a 50 percent reduction in manufacturing costs, a 50 percent reduction in unique parts, and a 66 percent reduction in development time.

Christ . . . concluded: "The purpose of benchmarking is to gain sustainable competitive advantage. Specifically, know yourself. Know your competition and best-in-class. Study them. Learn from them and be ready to adapt their best practices—how they do things."

Since Xerox's foray into competitive benchmarking, the practice has been increasingly adopted by a variety of organizations as a tool for change, adaptation, and growth. Can it work in higher education? Do colleges and universities compete? Are other schools really considered the enemy? Colleges and universities consider themselves to be unique organizations. Can this uniqueness and difference be sustained by measuring institutional cost, quality, and service performance against the performance of "competitors"?

BENCHMARKING IN HIGHER EDUCATION

Within higher education benchmarking is a relatively new phenomenon. Although the industry has been awash in comparative data for many years, very little of it has focused on key operational *processes* and the *outputs* of those processes. Traditionally, comparative data has been used to justify budget requests or legislative appropriations, to satisfy the ratio requirements of rating agencies, or to keep managers and boards informed about institutional revenue and expense patterns. This traditional comparative data most often takes the form of balance sheet ratios, revenues and expenditures per student, and other similar measures. In almost all cases these measures have been used to defend institutional growth, program expansion, or budgeting increases.

However, as the landscape of higher education finances has changed for the worse, a variety of "corporate approaches" has taken root in the traditionally rocky soil of many institutions. The combination of state appropriation reductions, slower-growing tuition rates, changing demographics, and numerous external demands by government and the public to "change the way colleges and universities operate" has created greater receptivity to various corporate tools for change. It is difficult to visit a campus these days without hearing of a Total Quality Management (TQM) or a Business Process Redesign (BPR) project. TQM and BPR, like benchmarking, were spawned in the corporate arena and have begun to creep into the lexicon of higher education managers as the financial challenges grow.

Both BPR and TQM share several basic tenets in their approaches to organizational change. They each have:

- A keen focus on *customers* in terms of service, quality, costs and expectations
- An emphasis on the *process* by which goods and services are provided to customers
- A focus on objective measurement of readily quantifiable items such as costs, transaction volumes, error rates, etc. as well as of what one individual has called the "soft stuff," such as customer satisfaction, timeliness of delivery, service levels, and quality.

In both cases TQM and BPR seek to optimize customer service and to minimize costs by designing cost-efficient processes that meet or exceed customer expectations. (Our delivery company example describes how the competing company had designed a process that was doing a better job of meeting customer expectations at a lower cost.) The primary difference between the two approaches is the speed with which the process change occurs. TQM provides more evolutionary change, while BPR provides more revolutionary change. However, in both cases the emphasis is on customers (the beneficiaries of a process), outputs (what does the customer get?), and the process (how do we deliver outputs to customers?).

The challenge most colleges and universities face is reorienting their thinking around customers, processes, and a *different* set of measurements. Institutions not only need to rethink what they do but *how* they do it and how they measure themselves. It is in this rethinking and reorientation that benchmarking can play a pivotal role in reshaping an institution's administrative and financial thinking. At its core, benchmarking is output oriented, with a clear focus on the quality and cost of the output as well as on the process by which the output is produced.

The traditional view of college and university operational costs has been functional and organizational. Institutional funds tend to be budgeted on a department-by-department basis, with a clear emphasis on *inputs*. The implicit and prevailing assumption is that the more dollars that are put into a department, division, or institution, the better quality will become. Hence the traditional benchmarks of higher education tend to be input driven (e.g., instructional dollars spent per student, students per faculty member, etc.). Few measures are output driven, and in many cases, the quality of the output is assumed.

If colleges and universities are to be sustainably successful in reshaping their cost structures, they will increasingly need to move away from the functional or organizational view of costs. The emphasis must move away from *inputs* of resources to departments and to the work and *outputs* of those departments. The input of dollars to a department enables it to "purchase" a bundle of expertise, skills, and materials. The real challenge is to determine what the expertise, skills, and materials produce, how they produce it, what it costs to produce it, and how well it is produced. Therein lies benchmarking.

To better understand and benchmark institutional performance and costs, it is essential that the key departments, functions, and processes be identified along with their customers, costs, and outputs. Hence a partial list of such items for a few administrative areas might look something like the chart on the next page.

The chart looks not only at the inputs of dollars to departments or functions but at the outputs of the department, the cost of the output, and the service level (e.g., average elapsed time). Having assembled this chart, one might ask (as one university executive has): Why should I care about the cost of processing a purchase order or an application for admission? To ask such a question is to suggest that one has no interest in the cost structure of an institution. It is precisely these types of activities that drive a significant

Dept./Function/ Process	Customer	Output	Cost/ Output	Avg. Elapsed Time
Purchasing	Faculty/Staff	Purchase Order	$26.00	11 days
Student Admissions	Prospective Student	Accept/Reject	$37.00	3 months
Registrar	Student	Grade Reports	$11.00	2 weeks
Facilities Work Order	Faculty/Student/Staff	Completed W.O.	$18.00	4 weeks
Personnel	Faculty/Staff	Position Reclass- ification	$73.00	6 months
Development	Donors	Gift Acknowledg- ment	$19.00	6 weeks

portion of the costs of a college or university. The payrolls of all institutions represent hundreds, if not thousands, of people whose jobs are to perform hundreds of these types of activities however basic or simplistic they may seem. The execution of these types of activities is what the input of dollars to a department is buying. And while the per-transaction costs may appear small, the aggregate transaction costs can be quite large. An institution processing 13,000 applications for admission at a cost of $37 per application will spend $481,000 on that activity. The same institution may handle 57,000 purchase orders each year at $26 per transaction for a total of $1.5 million per annum (exclusive of the actual goods and services being purchased). For these two activities alone, a 30 percent reduction in individual transaction costs would yield savings at $580,000 per year.

TYPES OF BENCHMARKING

The simple table above represents the first of several types of benchmarking that colleges and universities can carry out.

- *Internal benchmarking* creates a baseline of information that can be used to measure performance progress as improvements are made. Internal benchmarking can also be used to compare similar or identical processes within an institution. For example, in a decentralized, multicampus institution, how do admission application transaction costs compare between campuses? Grade reporting costs? Dining service costs?

- *Competitive benchmarking* measures the performance of the organization against its peers or competitors. The intent of competitive benchmarking is to find an external standard against which the institution can compare itself, answering the question "Compared to what?" Is a cost of $26.00 to process a purchase order good? Is a process that takes 11 days to complete a transaction sufficiently service oriented? Without a clear sense of customer needs and expectations as well as an external yardstick for performance measurement, it is difficult to tell.

- *Industry benchmarking* is similar to competitive benchmarking but differs in that the "net" is cast more broadly to look at a larger number of institutions. In both competitive and industry benchmarking the goals are to provide external standards for internal measurement and to identify the best operational practices that could be adopted or adapted at an institution.

- *"Best-in-class" benchmarking* seeks out those organizations with the best practices regardless of the industry. The basic criterion is: Who performs this activity best? As a result, a college or university might compare itself to an airline's purchasing process or a credit-card company's billing process or a manufacturer's facilities maintenance operation.

Each of these types of benchmarking can play a valuable role in assessing the performance of an institution and its many processes and work activities.

AN EXAMPLE OF BENCHMARKING

A good way to demonstrate how benchmarking can be applied in higher education is to provide a semihypothetical example:

Gift Processing at Hypothetical U.

The development office at a large, private, decentralized university raises approximately $115 million per year from approximately 50,000 donors. Fund-raising is done independently by the six professional schools, while undergraduates are solicited through the central development office. Although about 80 percent of all gifts are received at the professional schools and the development office, the remaining 20 percent (or 10,000 gifts) are received by literally hundreds of offices throughout the university (e.g., faculty, deans, fundraisers, coaches, etc.).

The gift-recording and acknowledgment process at the university had evolved over the years. The combination of old information systems, weak reporting capabilities and a decentralized fund-raising organization had resulted in a somewhat complicated but well-understood gift-recording process within the institution. All of the necessary information was captured by the appropriate individuals in the process. On average, a total of eight individuals "touched" a gift as it flowed through the process. Some assemble batches of gifts, others check to see if the appropriate fund number had been written on the check, while others record the gift in one of several computer systems used in the process.

Recent budgetary constraints at the university had resulted in some across-the-board budget cuts of the university's practices. The development office, in an attempt to keep the "front line" of fundraisers intact, had elected to reduce clerical and "back-office" support staff. During the past two years such staff had been reduced by 30 percent. Although the gift-recording and acknowledgment process still worked, it had become slower. But the work was still getting out.

Within the past year two key issues had arisen. The first was a slight erosion in the number of donors along with a leveling of gift income. The total number of donors dropped from 52,000 to 48,000, while gift income remained the same at $115 million. Most of the erosion was attributed to a slower economy and increased unemployment. The second issue was a growing number of letters to the president, board members, and other campus officials complaining that gift checks were being deposited two months after donor mailing and that acknowledgments were being made six weeks after the fact, if at all. The problem became sufficiently acute within the institution that the board chairman ordered a review of the university's gift-acknowledgment practices. Some internal analysis and comparative benchmarking yielded the following information:

Gift Processing—Performance Assessment

Gift Acknowledg-ment Process	Current Perfor-mance	Customer Per-ception	Industry Bench-mark	Best-in-Class Bench-mark	Customer Gap	Industry Gap	Best-in-Class Gap
Response	42 days	14 days	17 days	7 days	28 days	25 days	35 days
Cost/ Acknowledgment	$19	N/A	$11	$9	N/A	$8	$10

On average it took 42 days to acknowledge a donor's gift to the university at a cost of $19 per transaction. (The $19 included all of the labor "touch time," materials, and postage involved in the transaction.) With

48,000 transactions per year, it was costing the university approximately $900,000 per year to record and acknowledge gifts. In terms of response time, donors expected an acknowledgment within 14 days, a "gap" of 28 days from the university's current performance. The average response time within the industry was 17 days, and the "best-in-class" (which happened to be a large museum) was 7 days. Ironically, the data indicated that those institutions with faster response times had lower transaction costs. If the university could match the best-in-class statistics, they could improve their responsiveness by 35 days and reduce their annual aggregate transaction costs by $480,000. However, in order to achieve such performance, they would need to change.

The purpose of this example is not to describe what the university did to address the problem but to demonstrate how benchmarking data can reshape an organization's view of itself. In this case the data were strong and compelling, and could provide an important catalyst for change. Similar scenarios can be played out in virtually every financial and administrative function on a campus. Although every piece of analysis may not yield such dramatic opportunities, the exercise will provide campus managers with a new and different window on their operational performance.

BENCHMARKING EDUCATIONAL COSTS

To this point, the benchmarking discussion has focused primarily on financial and administrative benchmarking. However, the concept can also be applied more broadly throughout the institution. In 1980 Howard R. Bowen of the Claremont Graduate School studied the education costs per student at a variety of American colleges and universities. To his amazement, the differences in costs per student were considerable between institutions. Some of this variation could be explained by mission differences, geographic location, and institutional size. However, when Bowen accounted for these various differences, the variations in cost per student were still large. His analysis could not account for the differences even when the educational outcomes were similar. He concluded that his data raised more questions than answers.

At a very high level Bowen's work was an exercise in benchmarking. It tried to focus on educational outcomes and quality from the perspective of costs. Some institutions could achieve high educational quality at lower costs, while others were the reverse. As higher education continues to be attacked over the quality of its "product" (outcomes) and its overall costs, it may be a good time to revisit Bowen's work. Why do such cost differences exist? What causes them? Administrative costs are but one part of an institution's cost structure; instructional costs are another large and critical component.

Ultimately colleges and universities will have to address the cost-effectiveness of the teaching and research components of their operations. Administrative cost reduction will assist in mitigating part of the financial problem within higher education but not all of it.

During the late 1980s Boston College began a delicate but useful examination of academic department costs. The study attempted to logically distribute a variety of departmental expenses across several different categories of departmental activities related to instruction and research (e.g., teaching core curriculum courses, teaching undergraduate elective courses, teaching graduate courses, and research). Among the many results of the analysis was the calculation of costs per credit hour (a proxy for "output") for each type of instructional activity. The information enabled Boston College to then compare the cost per credit hour of large groupings of disciplines (natural sciences vs. humanities vs. social sciences) along with the departmental costs within those disciplines (e.g., history vs. English). The data were useful in assessing what course offerings might be scaled back based on changing student interests and whether additional faculty, when requested, were justified.

The effort briefly described above is a solid example of internal benchmarking. Although the cost data was valuable in a variety of ways, it was especially useful in comparing the resource utilization of various departments within the institution. Even though some departments cannot be easily compared in terms of resource consumption (e.g., physics vs. English), others potentially could be (e.g., German vs. French). This internal benchmarking could then be used to examine if substantive differences between similar departments could be addressed without jeopardizing the quality of instruction or research. The college felt that an important next step would be to capture the "benefits" side of the equation in addition to the costs (e.g., quantifying departmental reputation in academic circles, student outcomes, etc.). Boston College also felt that it lacked a data bank of comparative statistics (external benchmarks) to assist with the evaluation of internal departmental studies. However, even without the external comparative data, the college had successfully launched an academic benchmarking initiative.

CREATING A NATIONAL HIGHER EDUCATION INFORMATION BASE

The National Association of College and University Business Officers (NACUBO), in collaboration with Coopers & Lybrand, has established a national data base of key benchmark data for a variety of financial and administrative functions within higher education. The information base provides data and benchmarks for 38 functional areas (see table) ranging from purchasing to development to human resources to housing to admissions. Although it does not yet include academic department benchmarks, some consideration is being given to including them in the future.

1. Academic Affairs	21. Intramural and Recreational Sports
2. Accounts Payable	
3. Admissions	22. Legal Affairs
4. Alumni Relations	23. Library
5. Bookstore	24. Mail
6. Career Planning and Placement Center	25. Multicampus System Administration
7. Central Budget Department	26. Parking
8. Central Stores	27. Payroll
9. Collections	28. Police/Security
10. Development Office	29. Purchasing
11. Environmental Health and Safety	30. Registrar
12. Facilities	31. Sponsored Projects
13. Financial Aid	32. Student Accounts Receivable/Student Billing
14. Food Services	
15. General Accounting	33. Student Affairs
16. Human Resources—Benefits Administration	34. Student Counseling
	35. Student Health Services
17. Human Resources—General	36. Student Housing
18. Human Resources—Hiring	37. Telecommunications
19. Information Technology	38. Treasury—Cash Management
20. Intercollegiate Athletics	

The purpose of the NACUBO benchmarking project is to provide colleges and universities with current operational information and benchmarks as they consider various restructuring and cost-reduction initiatives. Approximately 140 institutions have participated in the project, which will continue for at least several more years. During that period additional institutions will be added, and the benchmark data will be refined and enhanced. Included in the database are a number of "non-higher education" benchmarks from business and industry to augment the information base. The overall goal is to provide institutions with timely, easily accessible information at a relatively low cost.

SOME RULES OF THUMB

For an institution beginning a benchmarking exercise, several guidelines should be employed:

1. *Clearly identify the department, activity or process to be benchmarked* so that apples-to-oranges comparisons are avoided. Key outputs, cycle times, and costs must also be well-defined.

2. *Keep it simple!* You are not trying to estimate the sociopolitical effects that might accompany the end of the world. Never-ending quests for the perfect comparison defeat the purpose of benchmarking and divert people's attention from the real objective. Benchmark statistics are not meant to be audited. They are intended to be pointers to superior practices and gauges for measuring the performance of your institution in light of customer expectations and the performance of other organizations. Benchmarking is only a tool, not an end unto itself.

3. *Don't try to rationalize why your organization's statistics are different* (e.g., "We're unique." or "Our culture won't allow it." or "Our policies require us to do it this way."). Find out why you are different. What can be learned from another organization? What can be adapted to your organization? The purpose of the benchmarking exercise is to find better ways of doing things, not to justify the way in which they are currently done.

4. *Don't limit benchmarking to your peers within higher education.* While partially useful, this approach will limit your knowledge of good practices and performance among "nonpeers."

5. *Don't limit your benchmarking to higher education.* What can be learned from other industries in terms of best practices? Many activities at colleges and universities are duplicated throughout other industry groups (i.e., purchasing, physical plant management, payroll, human resource management, food services, etc., etc.). Remember that the purpose of benchmarking is not to justify your differences but to find ways to become better.

6. *Act on the information.* Develop a plan for improving your performance. Establish goals, standards, and a timetable for improvement. Assess the cost/benefits of performance improvement, and determine the right approach for making the necessary changes.

If these guidelines are followed, a benchmarking project can be a manageable and illuminating experience, providing:

- An objective basis for improved operational performance measurement
- A tool for change within the institution
- A "pointer" to the best practices of other organizations
- A means to bring about change more quickly
- A vehicle for dramatic innovation

Benchmarking is not a panacea for what ails colleges and universities in the 1990s. It is only one of many practical approaches for reassessing how colleges and universities spend their resources. Benchmarking, committee studies, task force "white papers," and other analytical endeavors, while useful, only postpone the ultimate step: thoughtful and informed action. Benchmarking can be a vehicle for promoting substantive, change-oriented action within an institution by providing compelling evidence of the need to change. Properly developed and used, it might even be valuable in helping to avoid the creation of a new oxymoron in the public's and government's view: cost-effective education.

BIBLIOGRAPHY

Howard R. Bowen, "Cost Differences: The Amazing Disparity Among Institutions of Higher Education in Educational Costs Per Student," *Change*, January-February 1981.

Howard R. Bowen, *The Costs of Higher Education*, Jossey-Bass, 1980.

Robert C. Camp, *Benchmarking: The Search for Industry Best Practices that Lead to Superior Performance*, ASQC Quality Press, 1989.

Eileen M. Gaffney, "Cost and Productivity Analysis for Higher Education: A Look at the Boston College Approach," *Planning for Higher Education*, 16:1.

Kathleen H.J. Liebfried and C.J. McNair, *Benchmarking: A Tool for Continuous Improvement*, The Coopers & Lybrand Performance Solutions Series, CMA, Harper Business, 1992.

Barbara S. Shafer and L. Edwin Coate, "Benchmarking in Higher Education: A Tool for Improving Quality and Reducing Cost," *NACUBO Business Officer*, November, 1992.

Chapter 6

New College Leaders: Strategic Shortcuts for Short-Term Success

Nancy J. Dunn and Linda S. Wilson

Strategic planning is a fact of life on campuses. It is probably the most important process by which academic institutions' goals and objectives are set and against which their success is measured. However, strategic plans often focus on five- and ten-year time frames. In the 1990s college presidents often have less time to take effective control of their institutions and demonstrate success. How can new leaders increase their chances of short-term success? How can these new leaders know if their short-term plans and strategies are successful?

Joel Meyerson, Co-Chair of the Stanford Forum of Higher Education Futures, posed those questions to Linda Wilson shortly after she was appointed president of Radcliffe College in 1989. When I was later appointed Radcliffe's Vice President for Administration and Finance, Joel asked us to address those questions from the perspective of the president and vice president as working partners.

Our response is this chapter, which is organized in seven sections. In the first section we describe the expectations we faced and our knowledge of the surrounding circumstances when we arrived at Radcliffe. In the second section we describe three strategic shortcuts, borrowed from public and science policy, that we used to both increase success and measure it. These shortcuts helped us understand our circumstances better so that we could set objectives, establish an effective pace of early decision making, and assess early results.

In the third section we describe how the picture of Radcliffe's circumstances—its internal capacity and authorizing environment—emerged through the use of these shortcuts, and how we set our pace for progress in response. In the fourth section we describe six key operating strategies that emerged at Radcliffe in recognition of these circumstances. The fifth section describes those elements of our working partnership which contributed most to successful decision making in the short term. The sixth section describes some mistakes we made, principally related to the pace we set, and the lessons we learned about how to increase short-term success in the first year of our partnership. The final, seventh section summarizes the key points we make about improving the odds for short-term success.

We recognize that our experience does not provide the basis for a far-reaching strategy to increase short-term success or a set of tools to assess for intervention in the short term. However, we think that the key operating strategies that emerged at Radcliffe, and the lessons we learned, may be applicable to other settings and academic leaders. We also think that the strategic shortcuts we describe in the second section and the elements of partnership we describe in the fifth section are likely to be particularly useful to a new leadership team.

EXPECTATIONS AND CIRCUMSTANCES

Before new leaders act, they need to understand not only the expectations imposed on them by their various constituents but the key circumstances affecting their ability to live up to those expectations. Often, those expectations and the circumstances are in conflict. It is important to recognize the conflicts as early as possible in order to reconcile them.

In this section we begin by describing the expectations facing the new presidency at Radcliffe. Because the circumstances were not very clear to us when we arrived, we did not know the extent to which there might be conflicts between expectations and circumstances which had to be managed. We began that process of discovery by identifying the types of information we felt we needed to know in order to understand our circumstances.

Expectations of the President and the College

When President Wilson was appointed, the fundamental expectation of the Radcliffe Board of Trustees was that she and her senior officers would move Radcliffe forward in its mission. The board had four broad goals for the new president: to uphold and further the mission of the college; to facilitate women's participation and contributions to society through the college's programs; to support a 1977 agreement defining the relationship of Harvard and Radcliffe; and to affirm the value of Radcliffe and its independent programs. To do so, the president needed to communicate the college's evolving roles and functions to a wide audience.

The board expected the president to both serve the institution well and to manage well in carrying out these goals, and articulated standards for doing so. By serving well, the board meant affecting constituents in significant, positive ways and, in turn, increasing the value ascribed to Radcliffe and its purposes by the public. By managing well, the board meant that the president should develop and manage resources effectively. In particular, the board wanted the president to heighten the staff's quality of performance and productivity and to focus toward college goals and objectives.

Although both the expectations and the standards were shared by the members of the board, there were many different voices and views regarding the particulars of implementation. This was true not only within the board but within other key constituent groups. These views were strongly held and often contradictory, especially with regard to Radcliffe's role and commitment to undergraduate students—a longstanding and difficult issue. There were also contradictory voices about the value of Radcliffe's specific programs. Few, even among the board, really understood the college's individual programs and how they contributed to the college's mission.

As the president took office, the local community and the press persisted in questioning the continued existence and purposes of Radcliffe following a 1977 agreement with Harvard University. That agreement delegated to Harvard the day-to-day responsibility for the education of Radcliffe women undergraduates. The agreement was widely interpreted, outside of the Radcliffe community, to mean that Radcliffe had refocused its programs toward research and away from undergraduates, and that its continued participation in the education of undergraduate women was unnecessary. However, a significant subset of undergraduate women at Harvard participated in Radcliffe's programs aimed at them and urged the college to continue its role as an advocate for women generally and for women within the Harvard University community specifically. Many alumnae, especially from the classes preceding the 1977 agreement, echoed that sentiment.

At the same time, scholars across the nation viewed Radcliffe's three research-based programs—the Schlesinger Library, the Murray Center for the Study of Lives, and the Bunting Institute—as unique national treasures and the focus of Radcliffe's purpose.

In short, there was no unified set of expectations to guide the new president. At the same time, nearly all the interested parties wanted the new president to move quickly to assert Radcliffe's place in higher education. The capacity to serve well and manage well, therefore, depended on President Wilson's ability to simultaneously mediate competing directives for program emphasis, more clearly communicate Radcliffe's role under changed circumstances, and demonstrate Radcliffe's value in the '90s. Because the college and its constituents were eager for the college to move to its next stage of development, these tasks demanded equal attention.

The Need to Act and Assess in the Short Term

We started out by saying that a new president has less time today than in the past to take control of institutions and demonstrate success. Why do we think this? One reason is that while a new college president could once plan on a "honeymoon" period, recent trends toward shorter presidencies shift the planning emphasis to the short-term and toward immediate action.

A second reason is that important external factors place immediate pressure on a new college president. Examples of such pressures include changing student demographics, a persistent rise in costs over revenues, heightened public interest in productivity, and increased competition for charitable donations. And this is by no means the definitive list of pressures facing new leadership. Most new presidents are expected to act before the relevant external factors can be fully identified, before the institution's vulnerabilities can be assessed, and before strategies to address those vulnerabilities can be fully developed in a long-term strategic plan.

All of the pressures already mentioned—and more—come to bear early on in a new presidency. The pressures to act in the short term can be even more intense if an institution is in crisis, or if, as at Radcliffe, the institution needs a forceful affirmation of the present course or a change in direction. Given these pressures, an important early step was to mediate conflicts about direction and, at the same time, set the right pace for accomplishing goals.

Information Needed to Surface Conflicts and Set the Pace for Progress

Understanding circumstances is key to setting the pace for decision making. However, it is a fact of professional life, but especially for new leaders coming in from outside an organization, that important decisions need to be made without complete information. Acting decisively in the short term carries a high degree of visibility and risk for new leaders. If complete information will not be available, what information is essential to support successful decision making in the short term?

We think the essential information is that which surfaces conflicts between expectations and circumstances, and provides insight for resolving, or at least managing, those conflicts. The information and depth of analysis available to President Wilson on her arrival permitted the college to continue to operate as it had since the 1977 agreement with Harvard University but could not help reconcile the current contradictions in expectations, nor could it adequately support proposed new directions or refute them. The college had reached a new stage in development that required both a clearer historical perspective and greater understanding about leverage for change. The president needed to know the college's current obligations and vulnerabilities, its possible future constituencies, and the flexibility of its resources.

We needed to know the strengths and weaknesses of our staff and the facilities, but we especially needed to understand our programs—the interrelationships, histories, and the rationales for particular features. Even more pressing, we needed to understand the financial limits on our programs. While the college's revenue, investment, and spending targets had been designed to produce financial equilibrium, given the current set of programs, results were at variance with those targets. However, we could not readily understand the reasons for these variances because our internal capacity for analysis was weak: we could not ascertain trends or the basis for past decisions, much less model new program options.

Again, we knew the broad goals we were generally trying to accomplish, and we knew we were expected to move at a fast pace. But key decisions about program emphasis still needed to be made. To first model the implications of our constituents' different expectations, we needed to know what our resources were, which resources could be allocated or reallocated, and just how fast a pace of decision making we could effectively sustain. We knew if we misjudged the resources or moved too quickly or too slowly, the risk would rise that we would fail to achieve our objectives and our underlying goals.

In summary, we knew what areas we wanted to explore in order to fill in the picture of our circumstances, but we needed some shortcuts for gathering and analyzing that information in the short term.

The Value of Short-Term versus Long-Term Analysis

Strategic planning provides one comprehensive framework for setting goals, inventorying resources, and evaluating results. But new presidents need to act in the short term. They need ways to choose options in the face of competing expectations, poorly understood circumstances, and unresolved conflicts between the two. They also need to assess the success of their actions in the short term. Traditional tools of strategic planning have limited application for a new president acting in the short term. For example, we found two of the most frequently used tools of strategic planning—trend data and the strategic plan itself—to be of proven value in the long term but of limited value in the short term. Because they are in such common use in institutional analysis, we think it would be worthwhile to detour in order to describe their weaknesses as short-term tools.

Trend Data

The use of trend data to support long-term strategic planning is appropriate—the emphasis is on results further out on the planning time horizon, and so there is an opportunity to gather the data before results need to be assessed. Trend data are also useful for understanding results in the context of recurrent patterns. But by the same measures, trend data are not as useful when the planning horizon is compressed, or the issue being analyzed has little precedent. Trend data can take too long to develop, or there may be no trends that speak directly to emerging issues.

Further, while trend data are often available to a new president, these data often have more bearing on old issues than on the critical new issues that the new president is expected to address. Nevertheless, staff, and even the leadership, may be tempted to analyze older data and older issues for two reasons: it is easier to work with readily available data, and it provides a way to "do something" in the face of pressures to analyze and act. The rationale for doing so may even be that it is helpful to understand history in order to address emerging issues. This may be true, but allowing analysis to be driven by what data happen to be available can also result in a misdirection of effort if the analysis of newer, critical challenges is postponed too long as a result.

An illustration may make this point clearer. An example of misdirected effort driven by available trend data would be the choice to develop a response to a sudden loss in tuition revenues due to low enrollments through analyzing the growth of college budget line items of expenditure (for example, travel, consultants, or personnel) over the previous decade.

This analysis of budget growth over time might point out items of fast growth that can become first targets for cutbacks to offset the lost revenues. But more useful data would identify budget growth in terms of mandatory versus discretionary expenses or core versus incremental expenses, to guide budget cuts more strategically—especially if low enrollments might continue.

The first data set—budget growth in line items of expenditures—does provide at least for one year the answer to the question "How can we absorb this cut in funds?" But the second data set—growth in core versus incremental expenses—makes it possible to answer the more strategic question "What expenses can we reduce and still protect core programs or services?" The more strategic question cannot be answered by using the first data set. But in the face of pressures to act, it can be very tempting to think of existing data, such as the first set described here, as strategic even when it is structured inappropriately for the task at hand.

The Strategic Plan

Another traditional tool is the strategic plan itself. One of the values of a good long-term strategic plan is that it can set the parameters within which an institution can make choices for the long run. But dependence on such plans or the process of their development may also conflict with a president's need to act in the short term. For example, when plans inherited by a new president are outdated, the president's actions still may have to be reconciled to those plans for some time to satisfy original authors who invested in the strategic planning process.

On the other hand, when a president must initiate strategic planning or inherits a plan in the process of development, a usable product can be a long time in coming. The strategic planning process may allow a president to build consensus about goals, but it will also slow down the pace of major decisions in the short term. This is especially true if the process of developing the plan is highly consultative or if there is an emphasis on an iterative process of reflection, discussion, and drafting.

We use these examples to underscore that traditional planning tools have their limits in the short term. As a consequence, leaders sometimes forego planning and assessment in the short term altogether if they see that the trend data available are not strategic enough, or that the up-to-date results of long-term strategic planning are too far out of reach to serve their immediate needs. This may seem an extreme response, but its virtue is that it avoids basing action plans on inappropriate data or counting on short-term plans to emerge from a community-building planning process.

At Radcliffe we do use traditional planning tools to build our long-term plans. But we supplement that process with strategic shortcuts. These strategic shortcuts generate the information we need to clarify circumstances so that we can act in the short term with reasonable confidence.

THREE STRATEGIC SHORTCUTS

Once the board's expectations of the new presidency were conveyed, the president conducted about a year of intense internal review and exploration to understand the college's circumstances so that she could make informed decisions about program development. That process drew on traditional strategic planning, generated substantial amounts of data and planning documents, and is ongoing. However, we needed to develop immediate action plans, devise efficient interventions, and assess progress in the short term. In this section we describe how we used three strategic shortcuts to generate the information needed to guide these tasks.

As Vice President for Administration and Finance, I contributed to this process the informal use of two simple, analytic models that we will call by the shorthand terms the "rainbow" and the "triangle." Their purpose is to organize information in order to support the process of achieving objectives. These models are commonly used in class discussions at Harvard's Kennedy School of Government, which is where I came across them. In fact, they are in such common use that I cannot provide formal attribution. I imported them to Radcliffe as informal tools and will describe how we have used them there.

Briefly, we used the "rainbow" to organize our goals and objectives, which provide the basis both for setting priorities and for assigning responsibility for their achievement. We used the "triangle" to inventory our internal capacity, or resources, and to evaluate the college's authorizing environment, or the degree of support for a particular objective under review. We used this information to decide our pace of decision making.

To help us assess success in the short run, President Wilson also imported the notion of "multiple, partial, converging indicators" from science policy. This approach helps us assess success when the outcomes we want to measure are not clearly linked in a cause-and-effect relationship—that is, do not result directly from Radcliffe's actions—or when we are monitoring progress on the broad front.

These three strategic shortcuts stand in the middle ground between fully developed analyses, at the macro, long-term end of the planning spectrum, and a steady stream of informal inquiries at the micro, day-to-day end of the spectrum. We found that these shortcuts supported the "thinking on our feet" that became increasingly important as the time for us to act became increasingly compressed. If success in leading an educational institution means, in part, achieving goals in as compressed a time frame as possible, then these approaches can help.

Setting Priorities: The "Rainbow"

Given the large number of goals set by the board, the first technique we found useful was a prioritizing device. We describe this technique simply as the "rainbow" to facilitate easy recall. This device helps keep track of the many steps necessary to achieve simultaneous objectives and helps in performing triage when many task or issues command attention. Because it gathers key objectives into one easily recalled framework, it can serve later as a checklist for measuring progress using the notion of "multiple, partial, converging indicators."

To understand how this "rainbow" device works, start by visualizing a complete rainbow, from its top band to its bottom band. In the first, top-most band we "write" the institutional mission. In the second band we write the key goals which support that mission. On the third band we write the key objectives required to achieve those goals. On the fourth band we list the tasks designed to meet each objectives, and a fifth band can list sub-tasks needed to accomplish the tasks.

The reader may recognize from visualizing this model that the "rainbow" organizes goals, objectives, and tasks in the same way that is done in order to manage by objectives. The device also serves to reproduce the organizational plan, if the institution's units are organized around its goals and objectives. To illustrate very briefly how this might work in an organization whose units are constructed to support specific goals, think of the structure of state government. For example, if a goal is "to ensure the public safety," and responsibility for that goal is assigned solely to the department of public safety, then the goal and the organizational unit are very closely aligned. In that case, the organizational plan and the hierarchy of goals, objectives, and tasks can be mapped using one framework.

This neat mapping, very common in governmental organizations, does not apply to Radcliffe. The fact that it does not apply at a college is not unusual. Often, responsibility for achieving goals is spread across departments. It does tell us, however, that it will be harder to assign responsibility for achieving objectives than it might be when goals and organizational structure are tightly linked. For example, one of Radcliffe's goals is to advance scholarship in the field of women's studies. This goal cannot be assigned to one program at Radcliffe but must be achieved through the collaboration of all Radcliffe's separate programs, because they contribute important but different aspects.

We mentioned that by organizing goals and objectives, the rainbow also helps to set priorities. This can be done by agreeing at the outset at what level—that is, on what band of the rainbow—the president and other staff will principally function. Typically, the president shapes and markets the mission and ensures that key goals are met. Her bands, then, are the top two: the mission and the broadest goals. At Radcliffe the vice presidents and other senior staff oversee the accomplishment of tasks to ensure that the objectives supporting the president's goals are met. The vice president's bands, then, are those in which the objectives and main tasks are articulated. This division of labor is efficient and keeps efforts focused.

Neither the president nor other administrators should get caught in the trap of routinely taking on tasks too far down in the "rainbow." New presidents often get caught up lower in the rainbow's bands than they ought to be—for example, in carrying out the tasks rather than enabling, encouraging, and ensuring that key goals are met and the institution is on track.

Both new presidents and new vice presidents can easily fall into the trap of addressing all issues as they cross the desk. This may even happen in an effort to understand the organization better, in a fashion much like that described earlier when we discussed the misuse of trend data. But what may appear to be progress in resolving issue after issue is at best a postponement of action on the priorities needed in order to achieve key goals at an appropriate pace. At worst, it is a sign of "work avoidance," to use the language employed at the Kennedy School to describe the impact of working repeatedly on the wrong tasks or within the wrong level of the "rainbow."

If this "rainbow" device serves to remind leaders within which "band" they ought to operate, then it follows that it is helpful in delegating as issues arise. When approached with a problem or a decision, a president can mentally associate it with the appropriate band of the rainbow and so determine that an issue is one only she can advance or one that she should assign to others.

Setting Pace: The "Triangle"

Our use of the "rainbow" allowed us to sort through and choose some key priorities for which the president and I were responsible. Still, the list was long. Given the large number of priorities before us, the second technique that we found useful was one that helped us set the right pace for achieving those priorities. Another very flexible model from the public policy arena, the "triangle," was particularly helpful in surfacing conflicts between expectations and circumstances and so in setting and adjusting our pace of progress. By the "right" pace I mean that we had to hold to a pace that was fast enough to reassure constituents that we were serving well and managing well, but not so fast that decision making suffered or resources were depleted.

The "triangle" is imagined as a simple isosceles figure. Each of the corners of the triangle is named, starting at the top with "Mission Statement" and moving clockwise with "Internal Capacity" at the lower right-hand corner and "External Forces" at the lower left-hand corner. The mission statement is anchored by a brief statement of the particular goal and related objective you wish to achieve. In actual practice, usually only the objective under active consideration is stated at the top of the triangle in order to keep the following analysis manageable.

Next to the right-hand corner of the triangle the user constructs a list of the institution's internal capacity, or all the resources which can be deployed to achieve that objective. Next to the left-hand corner of the triangle the user constructs another list, this time of external forces. This list includes key stakeholders and constituencies in what we referred to earlier as the authorizing environment. This review is intended to systematically identify the factors operating for and against achievement of that objective. When the lists are complete, the next step is to assess each item for its relative capacity to influence the ability to achieve that particular objective. The reviewer can then weigh the balance of negative and positive factors to set an appropriate, sustainable pace toward achieving that objective.

Though simple, this model gathers, in one place, information essential to correctly assessing the likelihood of success in achieving the objective and for setting the right pace to do so. A benefit of capturing this information in one framework is that the comprehensiveness of the effort prompts the reviewer to think of more enhancing or offsetting factors than might otherwise be surfaced. Another benefit is that assigning relative weight to factors is much easier within that comprehensive context.

Finally, while each component of internal capacity and external forces is informative as an individual item, seeing them side by side can prompt creative ideas for offsetting negative with positive factors or capitalizing on strengths within either category. Had we captured all important elements of the authorizing environment and Radcliffe's internal capacity in one model, we might have realized earlier some important conflicts and managed to avoid some of the mistakes we describe in the sixth section of this chapter.

Depending on the objective under consideration, the authorizing environment can include individuals, institutions, and even societal influences. The list can be very specific or very general. A typical list of resources that make up internal capacity would include staff, funding, and facilities. Resources can also include key donors, volunteers, visiting committees, and so on—any resources the institution can deploy directly to meet its objective. Though these resources exist outside of the formal organization, we think of them as part of our capacity if they are willing to be deployed on our behalf. The lists can be very general to capture all categories, but good lists are specific to the matter at hand.

Example: The Graduate Consortium in Women's Studies at Radcliffe

To understand how the "triangle" model worked for us at Radcliffe, it may be helpful to consider the lists that emerged from an actual review of internal capacity and external forces as we considered fielding a new program. The president had chosen to establish the Graduate Consortium in Women's Studies at Radcliffe in support of the larger goal of strengthening Radcliffe's role as a major center for research on and by women. When thinking about how to achieve this objective, we reviewed our resources and the authorizing environment. In this case, the list of relevant resources included interested and available faculty, willing and qualified students, a highly committed president, available funding, and good facilities support.

In this review, unlike some others we undertook, most resource factors weighed in on the positive side. It is important to say, however, that there are almost always competing demands for the resources that are relevant to achieving the objective under consideration. These competing demands may threaten to undermine progress toward the objective, but they should be surfaced and addressed, not ignored. In this case, for example, the president's personal commitment to the consortium was essential because she is the only academic officer of the college. This meant, however, that other demands on her time had to be put aside or postponed.

When thinking about the authorizing environment, we considered the individuals and institutions that approve, advise, legislate, regulate, compete, collaborate, or might participate with us in the consortium. The point was to consider the perspective of all individuals, institutions and even societal influences like the public perception of value that could significantly affect the likelihood of a successful consortium.

Elements in the authorizing environment can threaten or support an institution's objective, but it is rarely an either/or situation. There are almost always contradictory messages coming from the authorizing environment. Like mixed signals in internal capacity, they should be surfaced, not ignored, and their relative importance determined. In this case, for example, the faculty were very enthusiastic, but deans from their home institutions were understandably concerned about faculty-leave issues. In thinking about relative importance, clearly the support of the deans was most critical.

When there is negative or cautious feedback from the authorizing environment, we need to deploy resources to change the overall level of support in the authorizing environment by enhancing support or neutralizing opposition. In this case, time spent by the president was the critical resource to bring to bear in addressing concerns of the deans of the home institutions.

Just recently, the consortium was formally launched with very enthusiastic participation by its member institutions. Its first course was oversubscribed by highly qualified students. We judge this program to be a success so far and believe that its success supports achievement of an important goal for Radcliffe. However, the pace at which the project was developed was slower than we might have liked because it was so dependent on a resource—the president—who was being deployed in many other ways at the same time.

To return from the specific example to the general discussion, the reason that a triangle is used to organize information about the internal capacity and external forces is because, as the above example shows, those factors are interrelated. For example, we have already mentioned that opposition in the authorizing environment can be offset by deployed resources. Doing so may improve the receptiveness in the authorizing environment to that objective. But it is important to recognize that resources are being depleted in the process. The authorizing environment and resources are not static but are affected by our actions in either dimension. To construct the inventory in the form of a triangle underscores the interrelatedness of the authorizing environment and the resources.

In summary, the "triangle" is an old but worthy strategic shortcut, especially for new leaders and leadership teams. If used with some regularity, it can strengthen the memories of new leaders or groups, so that they are less apt to forget some key constituent or adversary, or to underestimate or overestimate resources and thus mistakenly set a pace for achieving an objective that cannot be sustained. When he was dean of the Kennedy School of Government at Harvard University, Graham Allison had a sign on his desk that read: "Make Me A List of Everything We're Forgetting." The "triangle" sends us the same message.

Measuring Success through Partial, Converging Indicators

When we talk of measuring success, we often assume that we are referring to outcomes that can be quantified. But success can be very difficult to measure in the short term, especially if the outcomes we want are expected to develop over long periods of time.

Radcliffe's mission is to "advance society by advancing women." Even when a broad mission statement like this is supported by more concrete goals, such as "advance scholarship in the field of women's studies," outcomes may be too dispersed to measure, progress may be incremental across large numbers of people, or advances may be the result of collaboration rather than independent action.

Therefore, indicators of direct responsibility for success or failure of goals can be difficult at best to isolate, especially in the short term. To compound our problem, it is also at the very core of Radcliffe's philosophy to achieve these goals collaboratively, making it even more difficult to assess Radcliffe's individual success in carrying out its mission.

Having said this, how can we measure success with respect to goals like "advance scholarship in the field of women's studies"? First of all, we are mindful of the advice Peter Drucker gives to leaders of nonprofits in *Managing the Non-profit Organization*: "We need to remind ourselves again and again that the results of a non-profit institution are always outside the organization, *not* inside" (1990, p. 140).

We understand this to mean that it is not enough to point to tasks performed, money spent, or even opportunities captured and obstacles overcome as evidence of success. Though we use the "rainbow" as a checklist for tracking the subtasks and tasks that we feel we must undertake to achieve our objectives, and we use the "triangle" to gauge our internal capacity and our authorizing environment in developing plans to meet our objectives, we recognize that these analyses are only means, not ends. They do not substitute for serving well or managing well, which can only be determined by impacts on our constituents. We must look for results outside of our institution to determine if we are on track.

From her experience in science policy, President Wilson imported to the college the idea of making assessments on the basis of "multiple, converging, partial indicators." An example from the sciences illustrates this idea. In high-energy physics, where investments of capital tend to be huge and likely results are indeterminate in advance, decisions about which next large facility to fund often depend on an assessment of many variables associated with the proposers and prior projects: for example, citations received, the results of peer review, the number of important breakthroughs, or the number of secondary spinoffs.

None of these indicators alone can predict successful outcomes for future projects at a facility. But when several of them point in the same direction, they converge toward a potential. It is, in fact, through the very correlation of these indicators that the weight of evidence becomes persuasive. If that potential is positive or desirable, it supports making the investment in that facility.

When individual outcomes are too narrow, then multiple, converging, partial indicators can help sharpen foresight regarding outcomes and support choices about priorities. This approach, rather than a dependence on measuring very specific outcomes, may be the most appropriate measuring tool for an institution like Radcliffe, which acts more often as a convener or facilitator than as a sole producer.

How do we use this tool to measure success of the broadest goals of Radcliffe College? The answer is that we focus our assessments on a multiplicity of evidence. We have to be willing to accept, for example, that successfully advancing the field of women's studies, as well as, helping to improve the quality of instruction in the classroom, or providing very popular opportunities for women to bring research projects to fruition through paid sabbaticals, represent reasonably appropriate multiple, partial efforts whose coincident success indicate that we have furthered our goal of strengthening Radcliffe's role as a major center for research by and for women in a meaningful way.

Of course, the success of Radcliffe's specific programs in aid of that goal can be measured very concretely, for example, by looking at participation rates and level of focused donor support for that program. Many of our programs are very sensitive to market forces—that is, if not highly valued, they will not be used. High enrollment, attendance, and usage rates signal success. Increased response in the press and increases in gift income indicate that our message is getting through. As mentioned earlier, the consortium is a success, so far, by those measures. That means that when we assess Radcliffe's success on the broader front of strengthening Radcliffe's role as a major center for research by and for women, using the notion of "multiple, partial, converging indicators," the early success of the consortium weighs in as a positive indicator.

We do know that we will not ever be able to precisely measure our share of the overall success in "increasing research on and by women." Success in achieving our mission statement, "advancing society by advancing women," is even more difficult to assess. Therefore, we focus our attention on the goals and objectives bands of the "rainbow" where we feel that successful efforts can improve the probability for convergence toward, or furthering of, the mission. Note that we did not say *accomplishing* the mission but *furthering* the mission because we know that a mission statement like "advancing society by advancing women" will not be accomplished or pronounced a success only because of Radcliffe College's efforts, however successful. Furthermore, the mission is a continually evolving frontier, not a fixed target.

As we noted, early signs indicate that the consortium is a success, and that success serves as a partial indicator that we are achieving the larger goal of strengthening Radcliffe's role as a major center for research on and by women. And that larger goal, if we are moving it forward successfully along with other larger goals, can indicate success on the broadest front. In fact, many indicators do converge positively and give us the confidence that we are choosing to do the right things.

However, some indicators are not as positive as we would like. For example, there is still persistent confusion about Radcliffe's identity and purpose. At the same time, we believe that not all of these indicators need to be moving in the right direction in order to show us that we are succeeding. While small objectives can be attained and measured, big goals can only be monitored on the broad front. By turning to multiple, converging, partial indicators to assess progress on the broad front, we accept that as with economic indicators, general direction matters.

RADCLIFFE THROUGH THE EYES OF NEW LEADERS

We started this chapter by saying that expectations of the new president needed to be considered in light of the college's circumstances, and that we did not understand these circumstances well upon our arrival. Nevertheless, we needed to set attainable goals and objectives for the short term and to proceed at a satisfying pace. The challenges for us as a team were to understand the circumstances, intervene where necessary to alter internal capacity and the authorizing environment, and set a sustainable pace of progress that produced early signs of success.

One approach we could have taken is to conduct the inventory of internal capacity and external forces first and then establish objectives that were attainable in light of findings. Another approach would have been to determine the desired outcomes first and then assess the circumstances that support or oppose them with an eye toward active intervention. We chose the latter approach, in part because the board had already presented several specific goals that had received widespread support. We felt that though there were questions of implementation and emphasis to be resolved, the goals articulated to the incoming president by the board served as an excellent reference point.

Once our sights were firmly fixed on the mission and goals, we divided the work of inventorying the circumstances within which we needed to operate. This division of labor rested on the agreement that the president's job is to manage the authorizing environment to line up behind those goals, and the vice president's job is to line up internal capacity to accomplish the tasks and subtasks that are necessary to achieve the supporting objectives. When we each looked at the college's circumstances, our individual perspectives were framed by these responsibilities.

The View of the Vice President: Radcliffe's Internal Capacity

Even though we accepted the goals as described, it was still essential to review our internal capacity before moving forward. When expectations are high or information is inadequate and either time or money is in short supply, an inventory of resources is essential before setting the pace for achievement.

The vice president's role certainly includes evaluating the resources that can be directed at accomplishing the tasks to support the institution's objectives. To illustrate, a review of Radcliffe's resources highlighted several factors, some negative and some positive. In the financial area we found that though we were supported by an endowment which was large relative to the size of our operating budget, Radcliffe was "cash poor." We had contractual obligations to meet whose costs were soon to outstrip related resources. Radcliffe had recently agreed to a major change in how alumnae would be solicited for annual giving, which shifted the responsibility and costs to the college in new ways. And a major gap between income and expense was anticipated due to exhaustion of resources developed in prior capital campaigns. In addition, our financial systems were outdated, and our staff undertrained.

On the other hand, Radcliffe's programs were all of very high quality, the facilities had been well maintained, and the senior staff were dedicated, hard-working, and had been at the college for some time. In addition, Radcliffe had a large store of "symbolic" capital to spend, earned from its long tradition of excellence and advocacy on behalf of women's education.

The View from the Presidency: the Authorizing Environment

An inventory of external forces in the authorizing environment is equally important in setting the pace for achievement. The president's review of Radcliffe's authorizing environment highlighted several factors requiring prompt progress. The institution itself was unsettled by the fact that the search for the new president had been long and had concluded just one month before the end of the former president's term. There were continuing questions about Radcliffe's identity and purposes. In addition, the proportion of alumnae who attended the college after the 1977 Agreement (that is, those who had less opportunity to understand directly the college's role) was rising rapidly. The economy was slowing, and competing claims for charitable contributions were rising.

The president also noted important compensating factors in the environment that allowed us to move forward. These included a supportive board, a diverse but extremely loyal collection of constituent groups, and a widespread assumption that programs fielded by Radcliffe would be of high quality.

Despite the many positive factors that emerged from our respective inventories, we did not conclude that we had the positive factors we needed, and some to spare, as we set out to achieve our college objectives. Instead, we concluded that we needed to improve our circumstances by building internal capacity and the degree of support for the college in our authorizing environment. We recognized that we had to build capacity and increase the number of positive factors, even as we set out to achieve our objectives.

The issue for us as a team then became how fast we could hope to achieve college objectives, given the need to spend time and attention on building capacity and support, as well as on achieving the goals set by the board. Given the results of our inventories, we felt we needed to be even more cautious about setting a fast pace.

Setting the Pace

The pace of progress can be driven by the resources available, by a desired outcome, or sometimes by circumstances—predictable or unpredictable. A challenge faced by new leaders is setting pace when the quantity and quality of resources that can be brought to bear are not well understood. Another challenge is to manage the frustrated expectations that can develop when a desirable outcome drives the pace but rigorous standards for that outcome act as a brake on progress. A third challenge is when circumstances create pressure to sustain a pace that conflicts with the reasonable deployment of resources or credible quality control.

Given our relative lack of familiarity with Radcliffe's internal capacity, we were at a real disadvantage in deploying resources strategically. In fact, our pace was initially set by desired outcomes rather than by available resources, and this caused us some problems when it turned out that they were in conflict. An example was the president's request for proposals for new or restructured programs whose design must meet exacting standards for quality, appropriateness, and uniqueness before she would take the proposal to the board for support. One example of such a standard was that Radcliffe had to be the best institution to undertake the program. Such standards, while important, had the braking effect described earlier because the resources were not adequate to match those standards.

As time went by, circumstances began to affect the purity of that approach. There are only so many occasions for board approval in any academic year, for one thing, and there are only so many times staff can find time to rewrite a proposal to exacting standards. Letting the outcome—however desirable—drive the pace can generate frustrations or impatience with delays. In such a situation, either additional resources need to be deployed, or the standards need to be lowered to match the resources available.

Of course, sometimes our pace is set by circumstances—by events, predictable or unpredictable, which must accommodated. A simple example for Radcliffe's president was the recurrent need to produce a decision, make a proposal, or meet an objective simply to reassure constituents that the president was serving well and managing well. Leaders often find that pace is often set by circumstance, and not always to good effect. An example from the Clinton presidency is the keen media focus on what was or was not accomplished by the hundredth day of his administration. At Radcliffe we are grateful that our plans are unlikely to be unveiled by the media on its own schedule.

We found that at first, we were frequently adjusting our pace because the standards we wanted to meet for new or restructured programs were very high but the resources we could bring to bear were already fully deployed on current programs. We had to settle on fewer priorities to which we paid closer attention and to which we dedicated more resources. While we extended the timeline for a few key projects, such as the construction of the college business plan, we focused intently on building a campaign to shore up financial resources and Radcliffe's visibility and on making progress in the new area of program focus, public policy.

Adjusting the Pace

Once a plan of action is designed that takes into account the perspectives of the leadership team and their joint decisions about pacing, problems that develop in either the pace of progress or the successful accomplishment of tasks can be diagnosed through a review of either the "rainbow" or the "triangle."

For example, when the degree of success in meeting the objective is greater or lower than expected, leaders can consider whether the cause lies in the opposition of external forces or the inadequacies of internal capacity. That is, if the pace of progress is faster or slower than expected, this should prompt a review of the inventory. Perhaps there was a mistake in the assessment of actual resources—staff time to commit to the effort is less available than assumed, for example, or systems may be strained beyond capacity.

A really significant difference between the expected pace of progress and the actual pace of progress in achieving an objective can warn leaders that the pace of achieving other objectives dependent on the same assumptions may be affected similarly. For example, problems in analyzing the makeup of our student market could warn us that a project to analyze the capacity of tuition-based programs to cover costs will slow down as well. If the project needs to be completed before catalog deadlines force decisions about the offerings, this is a problem.

It is also possible that something unique in the authorizing environment has happened to hamper progress or affect availability of resources. Legislative action affecting levels of student financial aid or a sudden downturn in projected interest earnings might be examples that would affect constructing the budget but not affect concluding an analysis of tuition-based programs.

The purpose of pinpointing the cause or causes should be not only to adjust but to "update" the inventory to reflect this new information. Keeping the inventory up to date will help to inform many future decisions about pacing, since the authorizing environment and internal capacity may be similar for related objectives. It is also important to remember that pace is subject to changing circumstances. The initial decision about setting pace needs to be made carefully, and the sense of internal capacity and authorizing environment noted at the time. Otherwise, when variances occur between expectations and the actual length of time necessary to achieve an objective, it will be hard to analyze and make corrective adjustments.

KEY OPERATING STRATEGIES TO MAKE THE MOST OF FIRST STEPS

New leaders need to develop strategies for making the most of first steps. To be effective, these strategies should respond to the institution's circumstances. Our review revealed that Radcliffe's resources were in some cases of very high quality and in some cases needed immediate enhancement, but they shared the common characteristic that they were stretched thin in order to support current programs. With some exceptions, Radcliffe's authorizing environment was quite receptive to the idea of the college entering a new phase of development, but there was disagreement about what direction that next phase should take.

Given these circumstances, we devised six explicit strategies to make the most of our first steps. These strategies included simultaneously assessing and investing across a broad front; systematically considering "make or buy" options; acknowledging deficiencies and addressing them—but tolerating slow progress; making every move count for multiple purposes; engaging key staff as leaders and change agents; and using synergy to enlarge the impact and significance of our programs. These strategies are described in more detail below.

The first strategy adopted was to *simultaneously assess and invest across a broad front*, since the areas in need of improvement were interrelated and all were acute. We increased staffing and funding in many areas simultaneously to address areas most needing immediate enhancement. These areas included development efforts; outreach to students, alumnae, and the local and national community; program coordination and development; financial administration; and staff development.

The second strategy was to *systematically consider "make or buy" options*. Where appropriate, we brought in outside help to conserve the energies of the president and vice president for the issues only we could address. For example, we hired temporary expert help to develop data to support our business plan and campaign plan and to conduct searches to fill key positions.

The third strategy was to *acknowledge deficiencies and address them— but tolerate slow progress* (and the frustration of others) while we focused on the key problems. We had the grit to promptly address inherited problems and make changes in organizational structure and positions that were difficult but necessary to better support the college's goals. These efforts took energy away from new program development. We made these investments of time and energy because we felt that our board was willing to wait on outcomes from other fronts.

The fourth strategy was to *make every move count for multiple purposes*. For example, searches for new senior officers were designed to reach out to alumnae and other constituents and to develop internal community. A visiting committee appointed to assess the college's financial health and advise on college administrative practices stimulated internal analysis and self-assessment, provided staff development, and engaged the interest of key financial leaders from other institutions.

The fifth strategy was to *engage key staff as leaders and change agents*. We wanted to increase the capacity for decision making and simultaneously reduce administrative effort on the part of the president and vice president. However, we should note that we had to invest heavily in this strategy because it called on staff to contribute to the college in new ways. Staff had not been called on regularly to exercise leadership on behalf of the college, as opposed to their individual programs, and a culture of ad hoc, independent action on the part of the programs had not yet changed.

The sixth strategy was to *use synergy to enlarge impact and significance* by aiming to build a coherent college community out of a collection of interesting programs. In the past, each program defined its own audience, invited its own speakers, and set its own calendar. This "independent program" model generated a labor-intensive and expensive competition for resources and audience and resulted in a diffuse public image for the college. Many small, interesting events took place, but there were no large impacts and no coherent public program agenda. One effort initiated in the first year to enlarge impact and significance was the "conceptual calendar" project. The objective of that project was to unify college program offerings under the recognizable Radcliffe themes of research, education, and public policy.

In order to implement these six strategies, the president and I needed to change the authorizing environment of our staff by rewarding and supporting the steps staff took to support these objectives rather than those implicit in the "independent program" approach. We learned that while we were often concerned about the authorizing environment as forces external to the college, the staff very much saw their authorizing environment as shaped very directly by the college leadership. Understanding this, we could increase the odds of their success by making their environment more conducive to success. This might happen by delegating authority to them, moving obstacles out of the path, or reallocating resources to assist them in carrying out these strategies.

VALUABLE ELEMENTS OF PARTNERSHIP

New leaders need to find ways to maximize the positive momentum of their first actions on behalf of an institution. Especially in institutions that have stopped changing, achieving this momentum is difficult. When we agreed to write about success in the short term, we were asked to identify any ways in which we used our partnership to improve the odds of short-term success. There were four key steps we took that built needed momentum and allowed us to act quickly and decisively as a team in the short term.

Four Steps to Build a Leadership Team in the Short Term

The president's first step was to *hire senior staff for a set of complementary rather than duplicate skills*. In many colleges, as in ours, the president is skilled at day-to-day operations. However, President Wilson worked to stay focused on the broad picture—what the college was trying to achieve, when it needed to be achieved—and on maintaining relationships with trustees, alumnae, staff, and students along the way. She wanted to divide the labor, not duplicate it. In our partnership both of us had prior experience in addressing complex situations with high stakes and acute needs, and as vice president, I had a stake in the vision of the college. My first charge, however, was to free up the president from implementation responsibilities. The need for a division of labor may seem obvious, but in a small institution, it required discipline to work by this division of labor on a daily basis.

The second step was to *commit to collaboration between the president and vice president*. This commitment to collaboration not only allowed decision making to move at a faster pace, it improved decision making by capitalizing on our different perspectives. Because we had an explicit agreement that the president was to focus on basic agreements and principles and the vice president on implementation, it was easier to both accept and critique each other's actions. For example, I could engage efficiently in the give and take of negotiations to resolve longstanding operational problems knowing that the president would accept my judgments. The president kept focused on the basic agreements and principles but sometimes helped me avoid negotiating a near-term problem in a way that conflicted with underlying principles or long-term vision. While we set boundaries based on the division of labor, the emphasis was on developing shared insight, as described in the third step.

The third step was to *strive for shared insight*. We began to see that we needed an explicit strategy for working together fluidly to produce quick, successful results without heading off in different directions or deploying the same resources at the same time on different projects. We found that it was helpful to consider issues first from the separate perspectives of the president and the vice president, then by "trading places," and finally by joining those perspectives explicitly to gain shared insight. We found that our most robust analysis and problem solving resulted from this joining together of separate perspectives. For example, our priorities and circumstances were clearest when viewed explicitly from these perspectives. Once having acquired this insight, either the president or the vice president can better manipulate the opportunities and constraints in order to change the pace of progress.

The fourth step was that *the president set the standard and the pace of productivity*. At Radcliffe President Wilson repeatedly modeled the six operating strategies she believed would make the best use of Radcliffe's resources. This steady emphasis on the same set of strategies set the standard for our program directors. For example, she tackled many issues simultaneously, focusing on their interrelatedness as well as their acuteness. She made it a point to buy expertise when learning it in-house would have been inefficient. She identified deficiencies and held staff accountable for addressing them, but she tolerated slow progress on many fronts. She chose proposals with multiplier effects, worked to bring the staff along in the change process, and insisted that programs move toward internal and collegewide coherency. As a consequence of this role modeling, she generally raised the level of expectations for productivity at the college.

We found that partnership contributed to short-term success to the degree that it was coordinated, collaborative, and thus synergistic. While each of us had a principal charge, we were committed to the idea that shared insight would inform individual responsibilities better than would individual assessment and action.

MISTAKES MADE AND LESSONS LEARNED

All new leaders make mistakes. There were five mistakes we made to which we think new presidents and vice presidents may be particularly vulnerable. We describe the mistakes we made in very specific terms and then restate them in broader terms to make them useful in contexts other than Radcliffe's.

Radcliffe's president was being asked to redefine and reenergize an institution of longstanding traditions. *It was a mistake not to arrange for a period of partial relief from the full operating load at the outset of the presidency in order to identify and assess problems.* The president would have benefited enormously by the appointment of an assistant president for a period of six months while she undertook the necessary immediate outreach and internal examination, especially since the president is the only academic officer of the college. To generalize, our mistake was that we did not realize that one of the most important but scarcest resources in the college's internal capacity—the president—was seriously overdeployed.

The second mistake was *to not engage a consultant or temporary assistant to help construct an overall inventory of resources on an operational level.* For example, the president assigned a higher level of experience and sophistication to the existing financial staff than actually existed. This occurred partly because very little information about staffing, financial status, degrees of financial freedom, and so forth was available for presidential candidates. The president's initial assessment was overly optimistic, because there was no obvious evidence indicating otherwise. But because the financial condition of the college turned out to be a major issue, the lack of expertise dramatically slowed down our pace of progress. Our mistake was in deciding to "make" rather than "buy" expertise in an area that needed immediate attention.

In retrospect, the lack of key financial information at the start turned out to be a good predictor of later difficulties in generating and gathering information necessary to support a strategic plan. *It was a mistake not to recognize that the lack of key financial information meant there would be missing data in other areas.* Here the mistake was in not generalizing from one experience, where our pace was slowed due to inadequate information, to others. We should have lowered our expectations—that is, revised our view of internal capacity and adjusted our expected pace of progress.

Had we noted, as part of our inventory of the authorizing environment, the increasing frustration of board members with delays in achieving our desired outcomes, we could have deployed a key resource—in this case, board meetings—to communicate better. *It was a mistake to take the board's support for granted.* We should have presented the comprehensive picture, as it unfolded, to the board of trustees. In that way they could have seen simultaneous initiatives, comprehended the whole, and recognized and accepted that the length of time needed to achieve the objectives was longer than anticipated, and the pace of progress slower. Although the board started out supportive, delays had a negative effect. Put more broadly, our mistake was to forget that the authorizing environment does not remain static.

We had the vision and broad directions for the college, and some program plan outlines, but the articulation of the two was not adequate. *It was a mistake to overestimate the ease with which the public could understand and accept an institution with no analogue.* Again, in assessing the authorizing environment, we should have assigned greater weight to the continuing confusion and dedicated additional resources to articulation and public relations efforts.

Having the strategic shortcuts of the "rainbow," "triangle," and "multiple, partial, converging indicators" at hand did not automatically guarantee that we would read the circumstances, set a good pace, and assess results correctly. But having recognized these mistakes, our inventorying skills grew, and our inventory was better grounded in reality as a result. We assigned more weight to persistent obstacles and less weight to positive forces in the authorizing environment, even as we realized that neither the internal capacity nor authorizing environment are static.

Lessons Learned

There are four important lessons we learned as a new president and CFO, and they are these: triaging is essential; partial progress on many fronts can be effective; new initiatives may have to be fielded to sustain the interest of constituents; and leaders can afford to move forward with inadequate information if strongly supported by their board. These lessons, which are spelled out in more detail below, are really prescriptions for managing the pace of progress and the inevitable conflicts that surface between expectations and circumstances.

First, our experience reinforced daily the idea that *triaging is essential to maintaining pace and keeping priorities in order*. Internal communications, while essential to triaging, are difficult to sustain when the pace is rapid.

Second, *partial progress along a broad front can be effective*. The president and senior staff must see and act within the broader picture but also must be able to find satisfaction in small steps.

Third, the more coherent and focused the stakeholders are, the easier is it to focus college objectives on limited targets. *If stakeholders cannot be focused easily, new initiatives may be necessary to satisfy them.* These new initiatives necessarily require a dedication of financial and staff resources.

Fourth and finally, *new leadership can risk moving on the broad front without full information if the institution is basically sound and the board supports the idea of a unified board view*. Despite different perspectives and views, Radcliffe's board does function well as a unit.

As we move into our second year of partnership, these lessons serve as reminders and admonitions to monitor the quality of our communications, to find satisfaction rather than frustration in moving the front forward by many small steps, and to respond promptly to indications that key constituents need additional information or tangible signs of progress in order to stay focused and supportive.

What We Still Need to Know

Lack of information still does affect the pace at which we can define Radcliffe for the '90s and beyond. For example, we don't know enough yet to make really bold changes, to renegotiate some important agreements, or to be fully confident of the long-term wisdom of our strategies. We do know better what we need to explore further.

Benchmarks for Collaboration

Aside from the operational aspects we are still exploring, we have also come to understand quite clearly that given Radcliffe's operating philosophy, we could benefit from new ways of assessing the success of collaborative efforts. At the risk of complicating our efforts and the measurement of their success, we are interested in the process by which we achieve short-term success as well as in the results themselves. We would like to see the issue of collaboration addressed not just at the level of individuals but at the level of institutions. If, as we believe, success in advancing women's concerns in today's society is due to the collaborative efforts of many individuals or institutions, how can we begin to recognize and establish benchmarks for institutional collaboration?

Measures of collaborative success would be particularly useful to an institution such as Radcliffe that strives for cooperative interaction with other institutions, and whose role, because of its stature and size, is often that of a catalyst and pathfinder rather than producer. It appears to us that collaborative efforts within the educational community and between the educational community and the nonprofit and volunteer sectors are increasing as resources are decreasing, especially in the community services or social issues arena—but that few benchmarks for collaboration exist.

What works? What doesn't? We don't have a solution or a theory to offer based on our experience at Radcliffe. Rather, we are issuing a call for development of ways to measure the success of large-scale goals whose achievement rests on a multi-institution strategy.

The need for measuring success of collaborative achievement is not just an institutional concern but also true for individual professionals. If, as two of Radcliffe's institutional leaders, we design many strategies together, are there ways of judging the success of these collaborative efforts that are different from traditional outcome measures? Drawing again from the sciences, this is an increasingly important issue, as the nature of scientific endeavors and of the external resources available to scientists is changing. Internal university expectations and requirements for individual scholarly accomplishment do not yet recognize these changes.

Furthermore, university-industry collaborations often involve commingling of funds and cooperative, interdependent efforts, making it difficult to attribute responsibility or recognition for outcomes. For example, in the area of biomedical research, difficulty in assigning responsibility for successful research generates legal disputes.

Our situation is, of course, much easier to address; but we think we need to learn how to be interdependent, how to be collaborative, how to assess progress, and how to assess and recognize the accomplishments of partnerships in an environment socialized to competition. In particular, we need to know how to forge successful collaborations in the short term.

Benchmarks for Pacing

We also feel that pacing is an important component of short-term success. Much of what we have written about in this paper is the need to set a fast pace and the ways we have used strategic shortcuts to adjust that pace as warranted by changes in circumstance. Thinking more broadly about the subject of pacing, it seems to us that pacing might be a companion notion to benchmarking, which has, of course, received a great deal of attention. While benchmarking can be thought of as being about "how well," pacing is about "how fast." Benchmarking identifies an "industry-best" standard; but while both established and new presidents might set their sights on the same benchmark, new presidents face particular risks, because of lack of familiarity with the institution's resources, in determining just how fast the institution can achieve that benchmark.

We would welcome learning about the work of others that explores in more detail the issues of pacing we have faced as a new team. We do not need an "industry-fastest" standard, but we could benefit from knowing more about how institutions and their leaders establish a sustainable pace of progress.

SUMMARY

In this final section we summarize the key points that emerged in preceding sections. In "Expectations and Circumstances" we noted that in order to achieve short-term success, a new president or leadership team needs to be clear about the expectations and circumstances that affect them and their institutions. While expectations and circumstances are often in conflict, new presidents are expected nonetheless to move forward at a fast pace. To do so, they need to be able to assess internal capacity and external forces, then set a sustainable pace for achievement of objectives.

In "Three Strategic Shortcuts" we described quick routes to short-term analysis and assessment, drawn from public and science policy analysis, which we found helpful at Radcliffe. We then showed how we use specific measures to assess success of a new program, the Graduate Consortium in Women's Studies, and then how we take that success into account in using the idea of "multiple, partial, converging indicators" to assess Radcliffe's success in achieving a broad objective in the short term. If a president is expected to take action in the short run and to demonstrate success before goals and objectives are fully articulated, she needs ways to decide what to do first and the means to assess the results early on. We found that our analysis was enhanced by the use of informal models like the "rainbow" and the "triangle" and by assessing on the basis of "multiple, partial, converging indicators." We used these tools to set priorities, adjust our pace toward progress, and assess success. At Radcliffe both the strategies of long-term analysis and strategic shortcuts have been in use side by side.

In "Radcliffe through the Eyes of New Leaders" we applied the shortcuts of the "rainbow" and the "triangle" from the different perspectives of the president and vice president. Those perspectives provide the basis for setting, and then adjusting, the pace of progress toward accomplishments of goals.

In "Key Operating Strategies" we described six key operating strategies that emerged from our particular circumstances. Each makes the most of our internal capacity and authorizing environment in the short term. In "Valuable Elements of Partnership" we described four elements of our partnership that we feel improved our decision making and so the odds of short-term success. We found that the quality of our partnership was not only important to decision making but that it affected the authorizing environment from the perspective of the staff at the college. We found that the best strategies we could employ to set a fast pace in pursuit of our goals were those that encouraged both program synergy and shared insight.

In "Mistakes Made and Lessons Learned" we described mistakes we know we made in the short term and some important lessons we learned. We noted that the mistakes we made stemmed from not adhering to our own key operating strategies or by misreading our circumstances, despite the use of helpful and informative shortcuts. The lessons we drew serve as prescriptions for managing the pace of progress and for surfacing and evaluating conflicts between expectations and circumstances.

In the "Mistakes" section we also identified a need for additional insight on collaboration and pacing, which we feel were essential to improving the chances of short-term success. We think these issues have implications well beyond our experience as individuals at Radcliffe, and that educational institutions need to know more about ways to encourage, assess, and reward collaborative efforts at the individual and institutional levels. We believe that this need is increasingly widespread, and we look forward to the time when the work of others in this field can inform our continued efforts. We also recognize that the issue of pacing is an important one, especially to new leaders who need to show evidence of success early on.

At the beginning of this paper we posed the questions asked of us: How can new leaders, or a senior leadership team, increase the chances of short-term success? How can these new leaders know if their short-term plans and strategies are successful?

We have tried to answer these questions by describing our experience as a new leadership team with three strategic shortcuts for both surfacing and managing conflicts between expectations and circumstances and for assessing short-term results on the broad front. But throughout all of this we have tried to convey that what matters is not the strategies themselves. They constitute only tactics. What does matter, and what may find application in other settings, is that these shortcuts helped keep our focus on the mission and goals of our institution, helped to set a sustainable pace of progress, and at the same time, improved our odds of achieving short-term success.

Contributors ———————————————————

EDITORS

William F. Massy is the director of the Stanford Institute for Higher Education Research and is professor of education and business administration at the university. Massy was Stanford's chief financial officer from 1990 to 1991, vice president for finance from 1989 to 1990, vice president for business and finance from 1977 to 1989, vice provost for research from 1971 to 1977, and associate dean of the Stanford Graduate School of Business in 1971. He is author and coauthor of several books, including *Strategy and Finance in Higher Education*, *Endowment: Principles, Policies, and Management*, *Planning Models for Colleges and Universities*, and *Stochastic Models of Buying Behavior*, as well as numerous journal articles.

Joel W. Meyerson is codirector with William Massy of the Stanford Forum for Higher Education Futures and is a partner and chairman of the higher education and nonprofit practices of Coopers & Lybrand. Previously, he codirected the Forum for College Financing at Columbia University. He has served on several advisory panels, including the Massachusetts Board of Regents task forces on capital maintenance and tuition policy, and has taught at the Harvard Institute for Educational Management. Meyerson has authored or coauthored many publications, including *Strategy and Finance in Higher Education*, *Productivity and Higher Education*, *Strategic Analysis: Using Comparative Data to Better Understand Your Institution*, and *Higher Education in a Changing Economy*.

ESSAYISTS

Nancy J. Dunn is the financial vice president and treasurer of Radcliffe College. Her role is to provide leadership in financial planning and management of the college's human, fiscal, and physical resources as well as to help develop and implement Radcliffe's strategic plan for the 1990s. Previously, she served in the Kennedy School of Government at Harvard University as administrative dean, managing the day-to-day operations of the school, serving as client executive for a major construction project, helping set the school's strategic direction, and assisting in the negotiation of Harvard's first universitywide union contract.

Francis J. Gouillart is a senior vice president at Gemini Consulting, which was formed by the merger of United Research and the MAC Group, Inc., then the largest faculty-based consulting firm in the world. Gouillart is the Director of the Gemini Organizational Learning Division ("GOLD"), the Gemini arm responsible for global development and dissemination of new methodologies, as well as for the training of internal consultants and Gemini clients. Previously, he was in charge of multiple consulting accounts in the areas of corporate strategy, manufacturing and services operations, and the transformation of large corporations.

Sandra L. Johnson is a director of Coopers & Lybrand's national higher education and nonprofit practices, which coordinates the firm's college and university practice and informs clients of current developments in management, finance, taxation, legislation, accounting, and reporting. She edits Coopers & Lybrand's *Higher Education Management Newsletter* as well as other C&L publications. She is the author or coauthor of *The Decaying American Campus* and the annual "Agenda Priorities" column in the Association of Governing Boards of Universities and Colleges' (AGB's) *Trusteeship*. She is also the author of a forthcoming book on understanding college and university financial statements.

Sean C. Rush is a partner in Coopers & Lybrand's national higher education consulting practice. He has more than eighteen years of administrative, consulting, and policy-level experience with colleges and universities, state government, healthcare institutions, and service sector companies. He has been involved in financial planning, operations management and improvement, organizational analysis, management auditing strategies, mergers, and business planning. His clients have included Arizona Board of Regents, Boston University, Dartmouth College, Harvard University, Pennsylvania State University, Swarthmore College, Texas Select Committee on Higher Education, Tufts University, and the University of Minnesota.

Robert H. Scott is vice president for finance at Harvard University, a position he has held since 1987. He also is the director of several Harvard subsidiaries and affiliates, including Harvard Management Company, Aeneas Venture Corp., and Cogeneration Management Company. Previously, he served at Harvard University as vice president for administration from 1982 to 1987, associate dean for resource planning in the Faculty of Arts and Sciences from 1980 to 1982, director of the Office of Financial Systems from 1977 to 1982, and director of the Office for Information Technology from 1976 to 1980. Before joining Harvard, he held several administrative positions at the Massachusetts Institute of Technology.

Linda S. Wilson is the president of Radcliffe College, a position she has held since 1989. Previously, she was the vice president for research at the University of Michigan from 1985 to 1989; associate vice chancellor for research from 1975 to 1985 and associate dean of the graduate college from 1978 to 1985 at the University of Illinois; associate vice chancellor for research from 1974 to 1975, assistant vice chancellor for research from 1969 to 1974, and assistant to the vice chancellor for research from 1968 to 1969 at Washington University. She also has held a variety of teaching positions at the University of Sussex in England, University of Missouri, and University of Maryland.

Gordon C. Winston is the Orrin Sage Professor of Political Economy and Professor of Economics at Williams College. He is the codirector of the Williams Project on the Economics of Higher Education. Winston served as provost of Williams College from 1988 to 1990. His current research focuses on the economics of higher education, including collegiate wealth and economic information for governance and the time-specific modeling of production, consumption, work, and exchange. He is the author or coauthor of numerous journal articles and books, including the forthcoming *Paying the Piper: Productivity, Incentives, and Financing in U.S. Higher Education.*